REBUILDING CAMBODIA

Human Resources, Human Rights, and Law

Three Essays

Dolores A. Donovan

Sidney Jones and Dinah PoKempner

Robert J. Muscat

Edited and with an Introduction by Frederick Z. Brown

Foreign Policy Institute
The Paul H. Nitze School of Advanced International Studies
Johns Hopkins University

Copyright © 1993 by The Johns Hopkins Foreign Policy Institute, The Paul H. Nitze School of Advanced International Studies, 1619 Massachusetts Avenue, N.W., Washington, D.C. 20036-2297
202-663-5773

All rights reserved.
Printed in the United States of America.

Library of Congress Cataloging-in-Publication Data

Rebuilding Cambodia: human resources, human rights, and law: three essays / by Dolores A. Donovan, Sidney Jones and Dinah PoKempner, Robert J. Muscat; edited and with introduction by Frederick Z. Brown.
    p. cm.
    Includes bibliographical references
    ISBN 0-941700-79-8
    1. Cambodia—Politics and government—1975- 2. Political stability—Cambodia.   3. Human rights—Cambodia.   4. Law—Cambodia. I. Donovan, Dolores A. II. Brown, Frederick Z.
JQ935.R43 1993
959.604—dc20   92-38817
                                                                 CIP

Distributed by arrangement with

Public Interest Publications
P.O. Box 229
Arlington, VA 22210
1-800-537-9359

Table of Contents

Map of Cambodia — iv

Preface — v

I. Introduction: The Paris Agreements — 1
   Frederick Z. Brown

II. Rebuilding Cambodia: Problems of Governance and Human Resources — 13
   Robert J. Muscat

III. Human Rights in Cambodia: Past, Present, and Future — 43
   Sidney Jones and Dinah PoKempner

IV. The Cambodian Legal System: An Overview — 69
   Dolores A. Donovan

Appendix: Excerpts from Second Progress Report on the United Nations Transitional Authority in Cambodia, 21 September 1992 — 109

A Guide to Acronyms — 113

About the Authors — 115

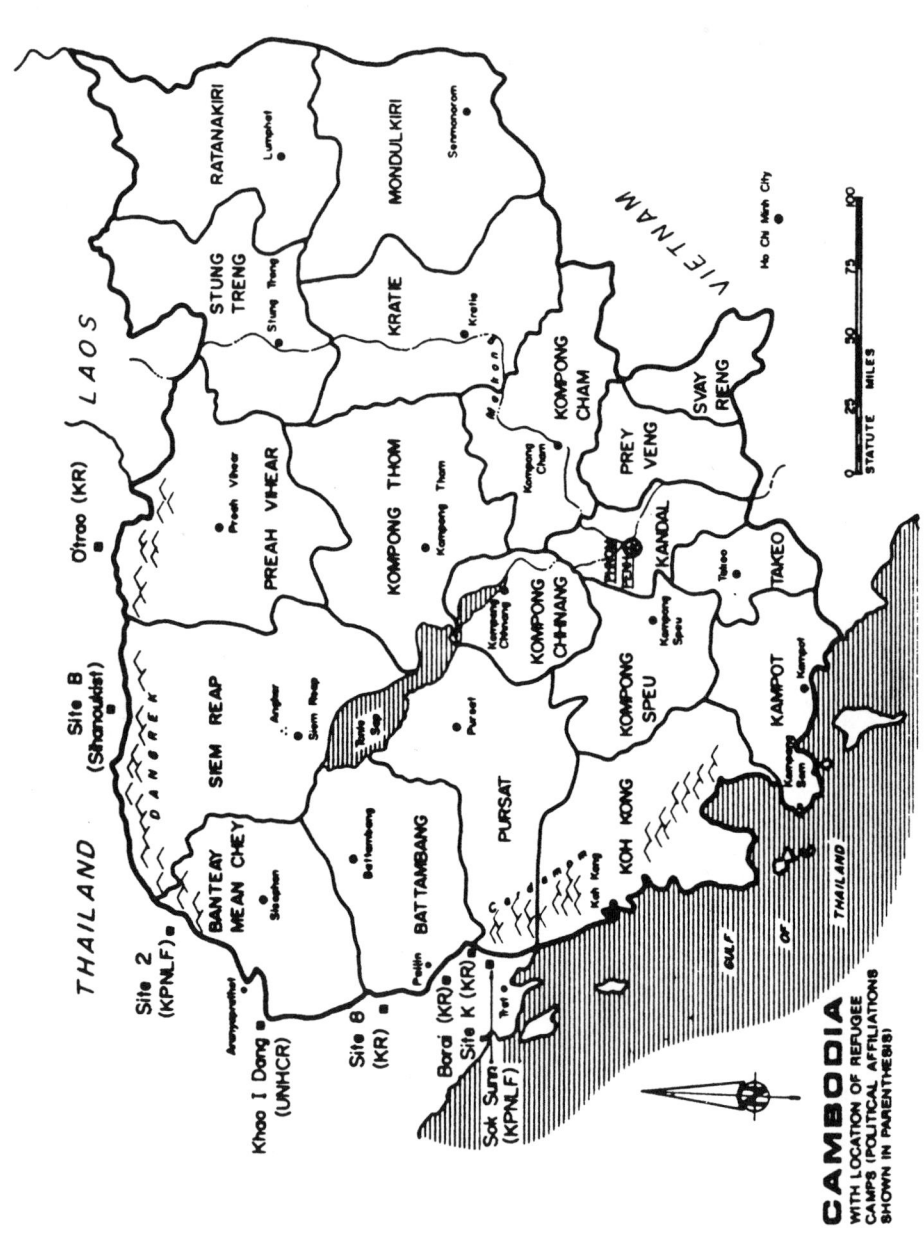

Preface

The situation in Cambodia is changing from day to day. As this book goes to press, the United Nations is grappling with decisions that will profoundly affect the course of the international peacemaking and peacekeeping process now under way. The United Nations process requires action on many fronts: providing security, encouraging political reconciliation, building an economic infrastructure from virtually ground zero, maintaining the genuine cooperation of Cambodia's neighbors, and gathering massive assistance of all sorts from the international community. At bottom, however, its success rests upon *human resources*—upon the availability, training, and protection of people.

The purpose of this book is deliberately limited: to analyze the Cambodia problem in terms of human resources, human rights, and the legal framework that is likely to be used as the model for a future Cambodian legal system.

All five authors have for many years followed events in Southeast Asia relating to their specializations. Their findings are based on separate visits to Cambodia in 1991 and 1992, during which they interviewed Cambodian officials and politicians, voluntary organization and nongovernmental organization personnel, social scientists, UN officials, and foreign aid officials of various governments.

Among chapters the reader will find repetition in references and supporting notes, particularly with regard to the United Nations' presence and programs. In essence, each piece stands on its own.

To help explain the extraordinary complexity of the situation the

United Nations faces on the ground in Cambodia, appended are excerpts from the "Second Progress Report of the Secretary-General on the United Nations Transitional Authority in Cambodia" (UNTAC), dated September 21, 1992, drafted by UNTAC's chief, Special Representative Yasushi Akashi.

The chapter by Robert J. Muscat had its origins in his presentation before the Council on Foreign Relations in New York in April 1992. The chapter by Sydney Jones and Dinah PoKempner draws on material used in the Asia Watch report *Political Control, Human Rights, and the UN Mission in Cambodia* (1992) by the same authors. Some material for the chapter by Dolores A. Donovan was gathered during trips to Cambodia sponsored by the Asia Foundation.

* * *

This book is made possible by a grant from the Henry Luce Foundation, Inc., New York, which funds the Southeast Asian studies program at the Paul H. Nitze School of Advanced International Studies (SAIS). The book is the first in a series on Southeast Asian topics to be published by the Johns Hopkins Foreign Policy Institute.

The authors wish to offer special thanks to Terrill Lautz of the Luce Foundation for his support of Southeast Asian studies at SAIS. Thanks also to Steve Brigham and Kim Neale of the Foreign Policy Institute, and to Maureen Towers and Mark Winter, for their valuable assistance in producing this book.

Frederick Z. Brown
Washington, DC
November 1, 1992

I

Introduction

Frederick Z. Brown

To understand Cambodia's plight—and the prospects for success of the unprecedented United Nations effort now under way there—one must look first at the years of bloodshed and political maneuvering that led up to October 23, 1991.

On that date nineteen nations of the Paris International Conference on Cambodia signed a historic document, the "Agreements on a Comprehensive Political Settlement of the Cambodia Conflict," designed to bring peace to a country torn for thirty-eight years by revolution, civil war, and massive outside intervention. The Agreements provided for creation of the United Nations Transitional Authority in Cambodia, or UNTAC, with a strength of sixteen thousand military and several thousand civilian personnel. UNTAC would command powers over the existing government that no United Nations mission had ever been given by the world community. Cambodian sovereignty would rest in a twelve-member Supreme National Council (SNC)—six members from the current Phnom Penh regime, two each from the three other parties—under the guidance of Prince Norodom Sihanouk, who would act as an impartial president. The head of UNTAC, Yasushi Akashi, would be empowered to make decisions and promulgate laws during the transitional period whenever Sihanouk and the SNC reached an impasse.

At the center of the Paris Agreements were four competing Cambodian, or Khmer, factions. The two main rivals were the Khmer Rouge, who had in April 1975 wrenched power from the U.S.-supported Lon Nol government and ruled Cambodia through 1978 as

Democratic Kampuchea, and the current Phnom Penh government, the State of Cambodia, made up of former Khmer Rouge leaders and placed in power by Vietnamese tanks in 1979.[1] Also signing the Agreements were the two noncommunist Khmer factions, Prince Norodom Sihanouk's party (headed by his son, Norodom Ranariddh) and that of Son Sann, a former prime minister. Sihanouk, Cambodia's once and future king, was the linchpin, again attempting to bridge seemingly impossible gaps of politics, ideology, and the cruel physical realities of an insurgency-ravaged countryside. After extreme pressures from their respective big power backers, the four Khmer factions signed the Paris Agreements. In truth, they had little choice in the matter.

The Road to Paris

The Paris Agreements of 1991 could only have been forged with the full cooperation of—and pressure from—the five permanent members of the United Nations Security Council. The roots of the Cambodia conflict were embedded in the global politics of the Cold War and in the bitter Sino-Soviet rivalry. China since 1975 had been the prime economic and military backer of Democratic Kampuchea (and a patron of Pol Pot, its leader, well before he came to power). There was little doubt as to Beijing's purpose: to prevent Vietnamese control of Cambodia and to demonstrate to Hanoi the geostrategic fact of life that China, not Vietnam, with its pretensions to an "Indochina federation," would ultimately call the signals in the subregion.

In 1978 the Soviet Union was entering the full flush of its burgeoning security relationship with Vietnam in the aftermath of the U.S. defeat. The Soviets and their Vietnamese allies supplied the newly installed Phnom Penh regime with arms, food, oil, and cash.

---

[1] The partisans of the Khmer Rouge refer to themselves as the "Party of Democratic Kampuchea," or the "DK." For simplicity, this Introduction uses the term Khmer Rouge in the singular throughout; subsequent chapters use Democratic Kampuchea, DK, as well as Khmer Rouge.

The Soviets had acquired valuable military bases in Vietnam on China's southern flank, thus exacerbating the Sino-Soviet rift. This new Soviet presence directly challenged the United States in the South China Sea and the western Pacific, and it troubled the noncommunist states of Southeast Asia. After 1978 China, the United States, and the six members of the Association of Southeast Asian Nations (ASEAN) began to lend varying degrees of encouragement to the three resistance factions, which, in 1982, joined in uneasy alliance against the Vietnamese occupation. In several senses, Cambodia had become a regional proxy war.

The United States, in 1979, had acquiesced in China's resuscitation of the Khmer Rouge and had voted for retention of Democratic Kampuchea's UN credentials. In cooperation with ASEAN, the United States had helped the noncommunist factions in exile politically and materially, yet had sought a low regional profile. Still smarting from its Indochina humiliation, Washington's cry was "Let ASEAN take the lead," and lead the ASEAN states did. Thailand gave safe haven to the Khmer Rouge, while its businessmen (and the Thai army) struck lucrative lumber and gem deals on the border. Singapore orchestrated a brilliant diplomatic campaign in the United Nations to isolate Vietnam and to ostracize the Phnom Penh regime. Indonesia, under President Suharto (a founding father of ASEAN in 1967), provided firm support to Thailand, which became ASEAN's "front-line state." Other members chipped in with training and money for the resistance. Britain and France, the two remaining Perm 5 members, shared the objective of resisting Vietnamese expansion, and they fell in line, though with reservations regarding the China-U.S. pact with the Khmer Rouge. A Coalition Government of Democratic Kampuchea, the CGDK, combining all four factions was formed to symbolize the resistance to Vietnam's occupation of Cambodia.

By the mid-1980s the Khmer Rouge's guerrilla campaigns throughout western Cambodia and the severe drain on the Vietnamese economy caused by the Cambodia adventure had convinced Hanoi that a neat military solution guaranteeing Vietnamese dominance was impossible. As early as 1981 Hanoi knew its claim of "irreversibility" was hollow; the effort began to strengthen the People's Republic of

Kampuchea against the day when Vietnam would depart. From 1986 onward it was a question of negotiating a compromise political settlement and determining the conditions under which the Vietnamese army would depart. ASEAN, led by Indonesia (with significant help from France), was the prime mover during a series of bilateral meetings between Prince Sihanouk and Hun Sen, the prime minister of the Phnom Penh government. This resulted in the so-called Jakarta Informal Meetings. Vietnam, all ASEAN members, and the other external parties to the Cambodia conflict participated along with the CGDK. UN representatives quietly shepherded the delicate process forward, with frequent detours and roadblocks thrown up by one party or another.

Although ASEAN's Jakarta Informal Meeting process failed to achieve a compromise solution, it was the essential preamble to a broader internationalization of the problem that would emphasize the direct participation of the ultimate power brokers of the Cambodia stalemate: China, the Soviet Union, and the United States (which remained something of a reluctant dragon on matters touching Indochina). The regional and global situation was changing. With military victory nowhere in sight and caught in a downward economic spiral, Vietnam unilaterally withdrew its army from Cambodia without extracting formal concessions from its foes. In Eastern Europe communist regimes were beginning to crumble. Soviet support for Vietnam and the Phnom Penh regime was wavering. But the killing in Cambodia's civil war continued.

In the fall of 1989 there was heightened fear that the Khmer Rouge, still militarily strong and well positioned in the western and northern regions of the country—and still supported by China—would take advantage of the stalled negotiations and the Vietnamese withdrawal to expand its influence and perhaps tip the power balance irrevocably. In this atmosphere Senator Gareth Evans, Australian minister for foreign affairs, echoing an idea put forward by U.S. Representative Stephen Solarz, proposed creation of an "international control mechanism" to rule Cambodia temporarily. In February 1990 Australia produced the first detailed plan for an international peacekeeping presence in Cambodia, in effect the initial draft of the

October 1991 Agreements and the prototype for UNTAC.

The disintegration of the Soviet Union in the summer of 1991 and the dramatically changed strategic relationships that followed were major factors in moving a compromise settlement closer to reality. The external powers that had sustained the parties most directly involved in the Cambodia conflict no longer found it in their national interest to continue on the same path; with the Cold War finished, the Cambodia game was not worth the candle. China, Vietnam, the ASEAN states, and Russia each had specific reasons for moving Cambodia from the forefront of their foreign policy agenda. The delegates to the Paris International Conference on Cambodia reconvened once more in August 1991, and in the succeeding months crafted the compromise document that was finally signed on October 23.

Lingering Dilemmas

It would be fatuous to claim that the Paris Agreements have actually resolved the Cambodia conflict. The Agreements lay out a plan of action by the Cambodian parties and the international community that, if followed assiduously, would create a stable, economically viable, new Cambodian state enjoying peace and a pluralist political system. This is the objective, at least. The key would be the *comprehensive* nature of the plan: the Khmer Rouge, because of its ability to disrupt Cambodian society, would be included in the peace plan rather than excluded. "Better to have the Khmer Rouge inside the tent rather that on the outside spitting in," so went the argument. Most important, inclusion of the Khmer Rouge was an imperative fact of life if China, with its veto vote in the UN Security Council, was to give its genuine support to the Agreements. Without China there would be no solution of any sort.

Comprehensiveness would also apply to the inclusion, on an equitable basis, of the relatively weaker noncommunist parties; that is to say, without intimidation by either the Khmer Rouge or the current Phnom Penh regime.

The Paris Agreements are a landmark accomplishment in peacemaking and peacekeeping for the United Nations and the individual countries that have participated in their writing and implementation to date. Yet they include, necessarily, a number of compromises and half measures to deal with deadlocks that could not be broken. And in light of what has happened during UNTAC's first year on the ground, it is starkly evident that fundamental questions regarding the "comprehensive" nature of the Agreements have yet to be answered satisfactorily, with regard either to the Khmer Rouge or the Phnom Penh regime.

Analysts of the current political situation in Cambodia (including well-informed foreign diplomats resident in Phnom Penh) differ in their assessment of the actual strength of the Khmer Rouge. Some hold that the Khmer Rouge leadership is split, that its middle- and lower-level cadres are demoralized, that its rank and file are disaffected and deserting in droves—in short, that the power of the Khmer Rouge to affect the peace process has diminished. Others maintain that despite some attrition, the Khmer Rouge remains as deadly a threat as ever, particularly in the long term. Another unknown is the extent to which China would choose, or would be able, to influence the future actions of the Khmer Rouge and whether China would consent to more vigorous UN measures to gain Khmer Rouge cooperation.

For purposes of this book, the authors assume that the Khmer Rouge remains a significant threat and that the dilemmas posed by its presence in the UN peace process have yet to be resolved, namely:

- Realistically, what can be the nature of Khmer Rouge participation in the process that leads ultimately to genuine political pluralism in Cambodia?
- If the Khmer Rouge remains unalterably committed to regaining sole power and to reimposing its barbarous regime, why should Cambodians of any political stripe (or the international community) give the Khmer Rouge the chance to do so?
- A UN process of fair, free, and open elections is unlikely to yield a Khmer Rouge victory or even significant minority participation.

Why, then, should the international community expect the Khmer Rouge to join such a process? Why would the Khmer Rouge agree to commit political suicide?

In his second progress report, UNTAC chief Akashi states bluntly that the continued refusal of the Khmer Rouge to grant UNTAC personnel access to the zones it controls or to commit its forces to cantonment as called for in the Agreements threatens to undo the Paris Agreements. While the Phnom Penh regime has cantoned (or given "temporary agricultural leave" to) 20 percent of its armed forces, and the Sihanoukist and Son Sann forces have furloughed proportionately more, the Khmer Rouge has steadfastly refused any cantonment or disarmament. It has denied UNTAC access to its base areas for strength assessments. UNTAC helicopters and ground vehicles have been fired on and roads leading to Khmer Rouge base areas mined. UNTAC has suspended further cantonment by the three other parties in order to avoid a military imbalance precipitating further large-scale fighting.

The Khmer Rouge is of course not the only problem. The Phnom Penh government has often been uncooperative when its self-defined vital interests are affected by legitimate UNTAC application of the Paris Agreements. Although a degree of accommodation has been established since October 1991, hardliners in the regime's Cambodian People's Party appear to be intolerant of the two noncommunist parties' existence. This fact bodes ill for creation in the future of a genuinely open society. In the competition for domestic political power, the Phnom Penh regime has a clear advantage. Although UNTAC representatives are now involved in many aspects of Cambodian life, the de facto *administrative* control of Cambodia remains with the government of Prime Minister Hun Sen. As yet, UNTAC has not been successful in creating the "neutral political environment" that, according to the Paris Agreements, is the core of the electoral process. The Phnom Penh regime has few financial or material resources; its personnel are poorly trained, low paid, and minimally effective in their official functions. Nonetheless, whatever governmental presence exists in the provinces down to the village level belongs to the central government and is more or less responsive to the Cambodian People's Party. It can be expected to promote the aims of the existing regime, despite the premise of the Agreements concerning pluralism and democracy.

The Cambodian People's Party is the lineal descendent of the Kampuchean People's Revolutionary Party, many of whose leading members (e.g., Hun Sen, President Heng Samrin, and Chea Sim, chairman of the State of Cambodia legislature and secretary-general of the party) are former Khmer Rouge officers who broke with Pol Pot and the central Khmer Rouge leadership in 1977 or 1978 and defected to Vietnam. Paradoxically, the regime includes a number of Western-trained Khmer technocrats at senior levels who evidently choose to work within the current government as the most acceptable way to make the peace settlement work and also to preserve a minimum capability for administering essential governmental services. How much power the pragmatic technocrats and the supposedly liberal prime minister, Hun Sen, actually have remains a matter of conjecture; the conventional wisdom is that Chea Sim and the ideological hardliners have the deciding voice on critical political matters, such as accommodation with the noncommunists, relations with the Khmer Rouge, and cooperation with UNTAC.

For its part, the Khmer Rouge charges that several hundred thousand Vietnamese remain in Cambodia as disguised soldiers or economic migrants ("settlers," in Khmer Rouge terminology) usurping Khmer lands. It charges that the Phnom Penh regime's administrative and police apparatus exerts a degree of control over Cambodian life that makes fair political competition for other parties impossible. It demands that *all* Vietnamese, however defined, be expelled and that the current regime's presence be drastically reduced and effective power transferred to the Supreme National Council before it will cooperate further with the UN peace process.

Although Khmer Rouge charges regarding Vietnamese "settlers" may be exaggerated, the noncommunist parties of Prince Norodom Ranariddh and of the Khmer People's National Liberation Front (now only partially under control of Son Sann) share this fear of Vietnamese influence. They also feel threatened by the residual power of incumbency that the Phnom Penh government enjoys under the operation of the Paris Agreements, even with UNTAC's large presence. Indeed, the government has shown little tolerance for organizational efforts of the other parties. Prince Ranariddh's party managed to open its first provincial office (in the western city of Battambang) only on September 30, 1992. Khmer People's National Liberation Front organizers have been harassed (and several reportedly killed in early 1992) while attempting to organize or open offices in the provinces. The degree to which Akashi and the UNTAC establishment, particularly its civil police component, can actually curb these abuses during the transition period remains a serious issue.

Hatred of Vietnam as Cambodia's historical enemy and of Vietnamese individually remains deeply embedded in Cambodian society; whatever appeal the Khmer Rouge has stems from its charge that the current Phnom Penh regime is responsive to, if not controlled by, Vietnam. UNTAC has begun to determine the voting eligibility of individual Cambodians of non-Khmer ancestry, primarily those with some Vietnamese blood, numbering perhaps in the hundreds of thousands out of Cambodia's total population of eight million. The Khmer Rouge objects to voting rights for such persons. While a pogrom against the Vietnamese community in Cambodia such as occurred in 1970 may not come to pass, incidents of violence against Vietnamese living in Cambodia have already occurred. More are likely in the future and could provoke a reaction from Vietnam that would threaten to undo the Paris Agreements, with obvious consequences for Cambodian society as a whole.

The Future

The Khmer Rouge's actions through the first year of the Paris Agreements call into question the Agreements' basic premise: that the Khmer Rouge can become part of the solution to the Cambodian problem rather than remain a source of discord and armed threat. One element of Khmer Rouge strategy is to draw out the peace process as long as possible on the theory that the international community will, in frustration, withdraw support from the expensive UNTAC operation. Will the Khmer Rouge agree to play the game under UNTAC rules? And even if UNTAC is successful in gaining Khmer Rouge cooperation in the cantonment and demobilization process, and then in the elections themselves, would the Khmer Rouge act constructively while a new constitution is written and a new government formed? Both questions are unanswered at this writing.

The United Nations' strategy is to give the Khmer Rouge faction every chance to participate in the peace process as defined by the Paris Agreements, a process that was accepted by all the Cambodian parties after prolonged and tortuous negotiations. If the Khmer Rouge chooses to be an outlaw, that will be its decision—and it will be treated accordingly by the international community.

On October 13, 1992, the UN Security Council put the Khmer Rouge on notice. The council voted unanimously that the Cambodian elections will go forward in May 1993 with or without Khmer Rouge participation. The resolution calls on Indonesia and France, the cochairs of the Paris International Conference, to convince the Khmer Rouge to canton and demobilize its forces, to permit UNTAC access into Khmer Rouge zones, and to join in the election process. The resolution did not suggest the use of force to obtain Khmer Rouge compliance but did hold out the possibility of some sort of economic sanctions if cooperation was not forthcoming. The resolution authorizes further consideration of a "consultative administrative body" to advise the Supreme National Council, a concept suggested by Japanese and Thai mediators to tighten control over the Phnom Penh regime's key ministries during the preelection period. And in an important move to stabilize Cambodia's struggling economy, the resolution invites the international community to make available immediately reconstruction aid (as differentiated from shorter-term "rehabilitation" assistance) rather than wait for an elected government to take power in mid-1993. Yet to be resolved is the question of whether an election of a president of Cambodia should take place before, during, or after the parliamentary elections in May 1993. The only real candidate is Prince Sihanouk; an argument can be made that his election as president before the parliamentary elections would

Introduction / 11

make for stability during a perilous period.

So the countdown has begun in earnest. The key time frames to watch are:

- By January 1993 we should have a clearer answer on the inclusion or exclusion of the Khmer Rouge from the electoral process, indeed the entire peace process.
- Meanwhile registration of voters will proceed apace and organization of political parties will continue.
- By January 1993 most of the three hundred twenty-five thousand Cambodian refugees in Thai camps will have been returned by the United Nations High Commissioner for Refugees (about one hundred fifty thousand had been returned by the end of October 1992). They must be resettled by January 1993 and then registered to vote.
- From January through April 1993 the UNTAC information and education program kicks into high gear and political parties campaign.
- In May 1993 the general election is held, votes counted, results accepted or challenged.
- In June and July 1993 the new constitution is drafted and the new government is then formed.
- Sometime after August 1993 UNTAC is supposed to end its transitional role. UNTAC would shut down its operations and depart. A reduced UN presence (some civilians, one thousand to two thousand military observers), however, may remain in Cambodia for two years or more.

UNTAC thus faces an immense challenge as it balances a host of forces jockeying for position on the Cambodian political scene, and not infrequently in deadly battle in the countryside. The dilemma of Khmer Rouge participation or exclusion (self-imposed or otherwise) remains unresolved. Some observers are convinced the Khmer Rouge will never consent to a procedure that almost certainly prevents it from gaining power through the ballot box and that it will conduct guerrilla warfare once more against whatever government is elected in May

1993. Other observers believe the Khmer Rouge is following a multitrack strategy: it will accede to UNTAC's demands, play by the Agreements' rules, participate minimally but relatively peacefully in the electoral process, and then await the departure of UNTAC to make its next move either within the system or outside it. In either case, UNTAC will be sorely tried, as will the political entity that is created by the national elections of May 1993. Clearly, the international community must continue to play a prominent and vigorous role in helping Cambodia reconstruct its shattered society. It is not unthinkable that the community will have to support the new government materially in countering a Khmer Rouge insurgency that could last many years. However the political scenario unfolds, a massive injection of resources will be required not only to rebuild the country's physical infrastructure but also to protect and develop its human capabilities.

II

Rebuilding Cambodia: Problems of Governance and Human Resources

Robert J. Muscat

One of the salient consequences of the end of the Cold War and the collapse of the Soviet Union has been the elimination of proxy wars in Third World countries. While this is a welcome turn of history, it has not put an end to local conflicts generated by internal disputes, or by old enmities between neighboring countries, ethnic groups, or putative nationalities. The demise of Soviet-style uniformity has opened a Pandora's box of frustrated nationalist passions in Eastern Europe and Central Asia. Most recently, the tragedies in Somalia and in the successor Yugoslav states have made clear how unprepared the international security and dispute resolution structures are for coping with the new generation of destabilizing and nasty problems emerging as characteristics of the "new world order."

Seen in the light of the hesitancy the United Nations and the major powers are exhibiting toward these conflicts in the postbipolar world, the situation of Cambodia stands out as a case of major significance even though the country itself has diminished in its inherent geopolitical importance. The provisional resolution of the Cambodia conflict reached in October 1991 is embodied in the so-called Paris Agreements, formally endorsed by the Security Council on October 31, 1991.[1] The Agreements establish arrangements among the conflicting Cambodian parties that are intended to effect a transition from warfare to a political solution based on elections, the promulgation of a new constitution, and the formation of a democratically based and legitimized government. The Agreements are designed to restore peace and stability to a country that has been devastated by two decades of civil war: under the Lon Nol government of 1970-75, through the Khmer Rouge terror and social destruction of 1975-79, and under a government (now called the State of Cambodia, or SOC) installed by Vietnam and guided, until the late 1980s, by Vietnamese and Soviet economic and administrative paradigms.

Under the Agreements, the four Cambodian factions—the SOC (which has ruled over most of the country and its population since early 1979) and the three parties that have rejected its legitimacy, occupying relatively small areas of western Cambodia near their bases in refugee camps on the Thai side of the border, the Khmer Rouge and the non-Communist Sihanoukistes (headed by Prince Sihanouk's son, Norodom Ranariddh) and the Khmer People's National Liberation Front (headed by Son Sann)—have undertaken to demobilize and disarm a substantial fraction of their forces, end their armed conflict, and submit their future fortunes to constitutional, electoral politics. These undertakings are to be carried out under the supervision of the United Nations Transitional Authority in Cambodia (UNTAC), at a cost originally estimated at $1.9 billion (but possibly running as high as $3 billion depending on how long UNTAC remains operational) to be provided by contributions from the international community.

While Cambodia is no longer a site of confrontation between Vietnam and the countries of the Association of Southeast Asian Nations (ASEAN), or a flash point between Vietnam and China, a collapse of the fragile agreement among the Cambodian parties could lead to a resumption of military action, and attendant refugee and human rights crises, that could destabilize the region again. Even if one takes the realpolitik view that the primary motivation behind the Chinese, American, British, French, and Russian (the "Perm 5") support for the Agreements was a desire to disengage and to downgrade the importance of Cambodia in the relations among the major players, these countries must support the process for which they are responsible—at least until the situation has reached a point at which it can credibly be declared as sufficiently viable to present little prospect of erupting again as an international security issue.

Other observers would go further. They would insist that the Perm

5 and the UN have taken on a responsibility to ensure that the Agreements lead to a situation in which there is no risk of the Khmer Rouge returning to power. In this view, the potential for the Khmer Rouge to legitimate itself through the very arrangements pressed upon Cambodia by the Perm 5 (and the direct support some of the Perm 5 gave to resuscitating the Khmer Rouge to oppose the Vietnamese military presence in Cambodia in the 1980s) forces on the sponsors a moral obligation to protect the Cambodians from a reimposition of Khmer Rouge rule. Of course, the designers of the Agreements shared the virtually universal view that in a free election the Cambodian populace would overwhelmingly reject the Khmer Rouge. Nevertheless, while the electoral process has been designed to minimize the number of seats the Khmer Rouge might win, the Khmer Rouge is almost certain to have some legitimated representation in the constituent assembly and subsequent parliament (assuming, of course, that it participates in the process).

The elections are supposed to take place no later than May 1993, before the next rainy season. There has been speculation over the UN's ability to adhere to this timing, owing to the delays in the refugee repatriation and demining and to the complexity of the electoral process, especially the nettlesome issue of the voting rights of Cambodia's inhabitants of ethnic Vietnamese extraction. The factions opposed to the SOC insist that Hun Sen authorities have issued bogus residency papers to large numbers of alien Vietnamese. The Khmer Rouge has used the Vietnamese presence as a justification for its refusal thus far to adhere to the disarmament and other provisions of the Agreements.[2]

Delay in the elections might be advantageous to the Khmer Rouge, giving it more time to discredit corruption in the SOC government and to use its legitimate access to propagandize the entire country. On the other hand, hatred and fear of the Khmer Rouge are believed to be near universal. Without benefit of opinion polls, observers who see a village here and a village there have voiced impressions ranging from certainty that the Khmer Rouge would garner few votes (outside the lightly populated western areas they control) to speculation that it could win as much as 30 percent. On balance, however, the presumption is that the elections will give the Khmer Rouge too little representation to win a claim on major participation in drafting the constitution or in the successor government or, in effect, a legitimated claim to work with international agencies in designing the rehabilitation process.

If the Khmer Rouge did emerge in a dominant, or even strong, position in a successor government, little if anything of what follows in this essay would have relevance. A more likely scenario sees the Khmer Rouge continuing to violate the Agreements and causing insecurity sufficient to make a rehabilitation process difficult, but not forceful enough to lead to total breakdown of the Agreements and a UN withdrawal. It is not the purpose here, however, to explore further the complexities UNTAC faces with respect to the security, repatriation, and electoral responsibilities under the Agreements. The assumption is that UNTAC gets the financial and political support it needs to shepherd Cambodia through to the elections, and that the optimists who expect the Khmer Rouge to be marginalized (and its strength to ebb as its cadres and noncombatants drift away, as China withholds further support, and as its earnings from border trade with Thailand are squeezed or cut off, perhaps as penalty for noncompliance) prove right.

Even under an optimistic scenario, however, it may appear essential, in the eyes of most of the players, for UNTAC to remain in Cambodia for some time after the elections, under a new mandate much reduced in scope and cost, to shepherd the successor polity through its inevitable trials. Sihanouk, for example, is on record calling for the UN to stay on for up to ten years. A minimal role would be to provide an institutionalized presence as a watchdog that would signify the determination of the international community not to walk away from its heavy investment in normalizing Cambodia.

It is apparent from UNTAC's role under the Agreements, and from the thought being given already to the longer role the UN may find itself in, that the Cambodian case is highly exceptional. For the international community, it is setting new precedents for legitimizing intervention into the internal affairs of a sovereign UN member, going far beyond the election monitoring in Namibia or the repulsion of aggression in the Persian Gulf. Whether Cambodia remains an exception or is a forerunner to the future evolution of international dispute resolution remains to be seen, and may well depend on the effectiveness of the UN's management of its powers and responsibilities in Cambodia, whatever the ultimate outcome in this particular case.

Under the Agreements, Cambodian sovereignty is vested in a twelve-member Supreme National Council (SNC) comprising the four parties (six from the SOC, two from each of the three opposing factions) and headed by Prince Sihanouk. While the head of UNTAC consults with and seeks consent from the SNC, the Agreements give UNTAC a wide berth, where necessary, to act independently and to make major binding decisions whenever the SNC reaches an impasse and Sihanouk is unable or unwilling to exercise the authority he has been given in that event. Sihanouk has been granted this authority in recognition of his unique role as former king and prime minister and as the only leading figure acceptable to all Cambodian parties and Perm 5 members.

What are these unprecedented powers and responsibilities? First, UNTAC is to supervise a military stand-down, including verification of the withdrawal of Vietnamese troops and the cessation of external arms supply, demining, and cantonment and disarming of the forces of the four parties, and then demobilization of 70 percent of the factions' troops. Second, UNTAC is to supervise, and move to control if necessary, the regular police forces responsible for law and order. Third, UNTAC must organize and conduct (not merely monitor, as in Namibia) national elections. Fourth, UNTAC will investigate complaints of human rights violations and undertake educational and other activities aimed at minimizing, if not preventing, such violations. Fifth, UNTAC will have overall responsibility for the repatriation of the three hundred fifty thousand Cambodians who have been living in refugee camps on the Thai side of the border. Sixth, UNTAC has coordinating responsibilities for the social and economic rehabilitation that is to be undertaken during the period up to the elections. The Agreements distinguish between rehabilitation and reconstruction, the latter referring to the presumed normality of development programs designed and coordinated by the sovereign successor state and assisted by the international aid system through its usual mechanisms. Reconstruction would kick in after the elections, in this case to be coordinated under a donor group chaired by Japan.

Seventh, and most intrusive, is UNTAC's role in civil administration. In order to ensure that the key instruments of the state that can determine the character of the elections are, in fact, impartially managed during the transition, the Agreements place control of finance, foreign affairs, defense, information, and public security in the hands of the UNTAC administrator, Yasushi Akashi, special representative of the secretary-general in Cambodia. For many of the other functions—in effect, of the SOC administration—the language of the Agreements gives Akashi wide scope for making his own determinations, after consultation with the SNC, if and when he should go beyond monitoring to the exercise of some degree of supervision or control relevant to his carrying out his responsibilities.

As noted earlier, there are reasons to expect pressures on the UN and the Perm 5 to extend UNTAC's presence even if the scenario of the Agreements plays out according to plan. The successor government may not have a firm hold on power. It would not be surprising if it fell apart from personal and factional division, or if the Khmer Rouge launched a major destabilizing effort, or if the political rivals fell back on the traditional practices of eliminating opponents rather than respecting them as "loyal opposition." At bottom, Cambodian history has not developed within Khmer society the precedents or natural bases on which stable parliamentary governance can easily be constructed. It would be foolhardy to suppose that UNTAC can press a single election onto this society and then pack its bags, and that Cambodia would then sail into the liberal, pluralistic, democratic future envisaged in the Agreements.

In fact, from a reading of Cambodian history, one might well conclude that the Perm 5 has chosen one of the most inhospitable places and times for this first experiment in international quasi-governance, with the UN playing role of midwife for a new polity. The problem is not one of merely bringing a set of national rivals back to orderly dispute resolution. Although Khmer ethnicity and culture are ancient, and the Khmer had a period of national coherence and imperial hegemony that reached its height in the twelfth and thirteenth centuries, Cambodia as a polity had undergone a long decline prior to independence in 1953. The society cannot be said yet to have the attributes of a nation-state. Scholars generally agree that the political decline has eroded Cambodia's social, even psychological, foundations:

> Caught between the expansion [of Siam and Vietnam], Cambodia's territory and population dwindled until the French established a Protectorate in 1864. Though Cambodia never disappeared as an entity, by the middle of the nineteenth century, only a sliver of the once great empire remained. In recent years Khmers have been acutely aware of this history. Indeed, their fear of being extinguished altogether as a people and a culture is not unfounded.[3]

Many would agree with Serge Thion (writing in 1987) that Cambodia's search for "a political system of its own" was more likely to succeed if based on traditional concepts of power and hierarchy than on an artificial parliamentary transplant. Referring to the continuities of Cambodian history—hierarchy, nepotism, corruption, and factionalism—and noting that political integration has never been achieved, Thion thinks that an effort to create a modern representative system "had better be forgotten as unrealistic and probably dangerous."[4]

David Chandler's summary of the past four decades is, in effect, another warning that the UN's transitional objectives are not likely to take firm root in a period measured in months:

> In less than half a century, Cambodian men and women were asked to alter and exert themselves to fit the interests of their leaders or the ephemeral concerns of other states. They were asked in the 1950s to be more democratic, in the 1960s to be more submissive, and in subsequent years, in a bewildering pattern, more republican, more socialist, and successively

more suspicious and more tolerant of Vietnam. . . . Few politicians after independence bothered with the day-to-day concerns or material welfare of the resilient, impoverished people on whose behalf they claimed to rule.[5]

Many of the same players are once again, under UNTAC's mandate, pressing their claims to resume national leadership.

Underlying Determinants

What are the prospects for achieving and sustaining social and economic stability? For bringing to birth a new state that can pursue governance with a normal admixture of aggrandizing politics and promotion of the national interest and citizen welfare?

On the positive side, although Cambodia is one of the poorest countries in the world, it has some obvious assets and strengths. While it will take years to clear millions of land mines from large arable areas, the land-man ratio is high and there is still much room to absorb population increases in the agriculture sector. Nearly 90 percent of Cambodia's nine million people live in rural areas. The resumption of village life, with important signs of the revival of the traditional culture (e.g., rebuilding Buddhist temples, resumption of customary religious holidays and ceremonies, the return of village labor exchange practices), should be reestablishing a fundamentally conservative peasant social base, built upon Buddhist principles of accommodation and nonconfrontation. With the horrors of extremism a recent memory, one might expect the society to prefer avoiding all fanaticism and to be drawn powerfully toward the central Buddhist ideas that preach the superiority of balance, of the Middle Way.

The Cambodians have also shown remarkable resilience. Despite its international isolation, the mixed blessings of the Vietnamese presence, and the denial of access to world trade or (non-Socialist country) aid, Cambodia has managed to restore a semblance of normality and a modest reconstituting of an economy that had largely been destroyed by 1979.

In the late 1980s SOC prime minister Hun Sen began an economic reform program aimed at moving the country from a command, socialist system to a market-based economy. The program has made some headway, especially in the return of collectivized agricultural land to individual family holdings and in the granting of ownership to the residents of urban dwellings. In one respect, the economic transition process may be simpler and less disrupting in Cambodia than it is proving to be in Eastern Europe and the former Soviet states. Although the beginnings of privatization of industry have created opportunities for corruption and carpetbagging in Cambodia, as in all the transitional countries, the industrial sector in Cambodia is quite small, employs a relatively small fraction of the labor force, and in general harbors much less potential for affecting the conditions the population at large faces, compared with the relatively industrialized economies of Eastern Europe. The economy has some prospects (in tourism and rubber, for example, and in the rehabilitation of the irrigation system) for income growth in the medium run, and some important options for resource growth in the longer run (e.g., natural gas and hydroelectric power). The SOC has also made a great effort to restore the primary education system and to expand the availability of health services.

A great deal of work must now be launched to gather basic data about the economy, its resource base, the state of its infrastructure, etc., in order to be able to conduct the kinds of agriculture, transport, and other sector analyses that are the routine stuff of development planning. There has been virtually no work of this kind for two decades, and almost all of the knowledge base that had been built up by the end of the 1960s was destroyed during the 1970s. The international agencies have started the survey process going, and we now have in hand the first broad look at the Cambodian economy since the World Bank's previous country study in 1969, plus some sectoral papers by specialized UN agencies. Prepared for the first meeting (in Tokyo, in July 1992) of countries interested in helping Cambodia begin its economic reconstruction, the World Bank's recent study provides the first extensive macroeconomic and sectoral analysis, based on SOC budgetary, financial, and other data previously unavailable.[6] The report gives a sobering picture of the problematic, negative side of the ledger and the obstacles that would make the rehabilitation process daunting even if a normalized and stable political and security framework were already in place.

While the economic policy reforms have had perceptible benefits—stimulating a revival of the private sector, creating more of an incentive structure for increased agricultural production, liberalizing prices and trade, enabling a reentry of foreign investment in such areas as tourism and banking—the process has far to go and is, almost inevitably, generating new transitional problems and highlighting the extraordinary weaknesses of the institutional framework. The absence of a modern legal system, the informal nature of the new ad hoc economic and administrative rules of the game, the remaining trade restrictions, the primitive financial system—these and other problems mark a transition process that will take time and persistent policy formation and direction to set the stage for modern economic development. Meanwhile, the process is messy. It is producing a small group of conspicuous economic winners. The withdrawal of the state from economic activities more likely to thrive under private ownership has opened the door to favoritism, speculation, and corruption. The long-term benefits of the transition process are likely to be earned at a short-term price of exploitation that is already grist for the Khmer Rouge mill. The process is further complicated by the problems of reabsorbing the returning refugees and the soldiers being demobilized.

The vigorous revival of private sector activity in Phnom Penh and a few other urban centers has given rise to an exaggerated impression of general economic vigor. The building and refurbishing boom in the capital has been based on the infusion of demand for office and residential accommodation by international agencies. Much of the trade expansion of the past two years has comprised entrepôt movement of goods imported from Thailand and Singapore and smuggled out to Vietnam. When Vietnam's external trade is fully normalized, this entrepôt trade may lose its economic rationale. The purchasing power the UNTAC operation will pump into the Cambodian economy will be an important stimulus for the private sector, but a source of deflation when it is withdrawn as planned during the third quarter of 1993. The revival of private economic activity will also be hampered by the dilapidated condition of the country's transport and other economic infrastructure.

The policy transition of the past year, in particular, has had destabilizing macroeconomic effects, including a sharp inflation, wild swings, and depreciation in the value of the currency. According to the World Bank report, the basic source of this destabilization has been the deterioration of SOC government finances. The economic reforms have slashed the revenues the SOC formerly received from the state enterprise sector, now increasingly deprived of monopoly pricing and other distorting practices that underlay its previous ability to contribute "profits" to the central budget. The SOC has also imposed implicit taxation on the general public by buying rice and other domestic goods at enforced below-market prices. Elimination of this practice, an essential step in moving to a market economy, has raised the budget cost of government procurement. New taxes on rising private sector activity have thus far not offset even the drop in state enterprise revenue. The budget deficit was further enlarged when the Soviet Union canceled its economic aid in 1991.

In an effort to maintain its defense and other expenditure needs, the SOC resorted to printing more money under an expansion that rapidly inflated prices. Even so, according to the World Bank:

> As high as it was, the available monetary financing became insufficient in 1991 to cover more than half the budgetary gap; the budget went in arrears for the remaining 20.0 percent of expenditures. Wage payments to the civil service, as well as to military personnel, have become sporadic. In brief, owing to the growing fiscal crisis, key infrastructures, already crumbling under the weight of years, are no longer being maintained, civil servants are walking out of essential services, and obviously no expansion activities are being undertaken, or even planned, by the administration to accommodate the new demands placed on these infrastructures and services by the United Nations operation and the resettlement of displaced populations.[7]

The erosion, if not collapse, of health and education services has been especially acute, as large numbers of workers and teachers remained unpaid for months, and as the funds for drugs, school materials, and essential supplies dried up.

The prospect that this erosion would have long-term social and economic consequences if not reversed, and in the short-term would destabilize the society and play into the hands of the Khmer Rouge, elicited an unexpected response at the Tokyo meeting, with the promise of large donations, including funds to be allocated to budget support of the SOC bureaucracy. Absent sufficient funds, UNTAC would have been put in the position of presiding, as a transitional caretaker, over a set of essential services faced with certain collapse.

Managing a State

There are practical reasons for concern over Cambodia's capacity to design a new policy framework, create the institutions of a modern state and economy, and manage a rehabilitation and development process. The successor government will inherit an administrative structure and civil service that is ill suited to the daunting tasks it will face. Besides the weaknesses of public administration one finds in most underdeveloped countries, Cambodia's administration suffers from a severe shortage of skills, owing to the destruction and emigration of the educated during the 1970s and the subsequent isolation from external aid and training opportunities (outside Vietnam and Eastern Europe).

The World Bank study proposes a number of steps to begin reorganizing the administration and strengthening its capacities. Critical to this effort and to future performance will be the task of creating technocratic leadership. The World Bank assumes that government performance will depend on some one thousand to fifteen hundred key positions. If the problems of the major financial and career disincentives can be resolved, however, the task of filling key positions with effective personnel and making the administration minimally effective for development management may be less formidable than a recital of current weaknesses suggests.

It is instructive to recall how weak were most of the administrations of the now relatively successful developing countries of the region (e.g., South Korea, Indonesia, Thailand) back in the 1950s and 1960s, when they were launching their modern development. Although the bureaucracies of some of these well-performing economies have not been models of efficiency and probity, they have overseen and promoted the most dynamic growth performances of the Third World. The political masters in these countries, by and large, have allowed their technocratic elites substantial authority over the development process. This has been true especially in the management of economic and financial policy. These latter key functions typically can be managed by a small core of senior technocrats.

In the case of Thailand, there were as few as a dozen or so senior technocrats (plus some well-trained juniors quickly put in responsible positions) in the mid-1950s. With outside technical assistance and moral support, this core set the basic policy framework, managed key policy and infrastructure agencies, and set the intellectual and professional tone for the larger technocratic buildup that followed. It was not until the 1960s that the return flow of young overseas-trained Thais rose into the many hundreds a year. This experience suggests that Cambodia, with its much smaller population and its much less complex economy, has a core technocratic need that may be measured in scores, rising to the low hundreds for a number of years.

These considerations point to a strategic perspective, respecting public administration and education, that appears to have been missed thus far in the first round of studies. In this perspective the professionalization of the core of Cambodia's state and development management—assuming Cambodian politics adopts the lesson from its ASEAN and East Asian neighbors—may be achievable over a ten- to fifteen-year period through a sequential program of (1) strengthening the current system of placing gifted students in special classes through competitive entry; (2) creating a single, first-class secondary school whose graduates could enter reputable universities overseas; (3)

establishing an aid-funded overseas university training program in development management disciplines for qualified secondary graduates; and (4) adopting a set of requirements and incentives to minimize brain-drain losses.

Over time the strengthening of local education (including tertiary institutions such as the Institute of Economics) will reduce the need for foreign training. The higher education institutions of Cambodia need thorough overhaul. After total destruction by the Khmer Rouge, a few have been reconstituted based largely on Vietnamese and Soviet instructors, books, and curricula. Most of these instructors have now left, French is replacing Vietnamese and Russian as the foreign language of instruction, and efforts are being made to revise the curricula and acquire some useful books and other teaching materials still in very short supply. While these schools are being strengthened, the most able students, secondary and tertiary, could be sent to schools abroad. Training in ASEAN schools would have obvious cost and other advantages. At the same time, it is important that a future Cambodian elite be socialized, through its educational experience, to the values of professionalism and social responsibility that have underlain the performance of the ASEAN and other technocratic classes.

If integration into the regional economy, economic relations with Japan, and a constructive foreign policy with the mostly non-French-speaking countries of the region are to be major elements of future Cambodian government operations, English should be at least equal with French as a foreign language of instruction, not just a secondary language to be studied. There will be sensitivities to overcome on the language issues. Younger Cambodians appear to favor learning English, while an older generation knows only French as a second language. Meanwhile, French technical assistance has been the first on the ground for several institutions.

Since Cambodian development management will be one of the scarcest resources in the near future, it is important to consider ways in which this resource can be economized while a longer-term, capacity-building program is unfolding. (Recent visitors to SOC ministries have found offices virtually deserted, while UNTAC has warned that the recurrent absences of Cambodian decision makers spells excessive dependence on foreigners.) Public administration expertise, for example, could examine the operations of public sector units and recommend changes that would enhance the reach and effectiveness of senior management. Special attention should be given to the provincial and district-level administrations. Many of the public sector field functions are already, perforce, decentralized to the provinces and districts. Decentralization could be an important asset if it operates to encourage the emergence of administrative capability wherever it may be found. Specialized institutional in-service training proved to be a major factor that turned Thailand's local administrative levels into development instruments, and might serve as a model for Cambodia.

There is a widely held view in Phnom Penh that the inrush of external agencies is already dangerously overloading the existing administrative capacities and upstaging the senior Cambodian officials. This would be an ironic and most unfortunate result of the onset of efforts intended to produce the exact opposite impact. The donors should be exploring ways of minimizing the local administrative capacity that is preempted by the aid process itself. Specious data requirements and exactitude in program and project planning, for example, should be avoided as well as complexity and duplication in coordination and execution arrangements. Documentation requirements should be simplified and fulfilled as much as possible by the aid agencies themselves. Projects should be packaged so as to reduce to a minimum the number of management units for which Cambodian managers will be responsible. To avoid adding excessive complexity or proliferating options that could diffuse administrative attention, it may be wise to limit the numbers of models or pilot schemes and to focus on proving out limited numbers of interventions and approaches, and on testing replicability and scaling up.

Another economizing principle should be to limit the creation of new institutions, phasing in such entities over time so as to avoid excessive pressure on management cadres while such cadres are still in short supply. It will be important to apply hard-nosed criteria to proposals for new entities and to develop some system of priorities.

With all of Cambodia's institutions having been gutted or destroyed a mere dozen years ago, it seems prima facie evident that *everything* needs to be done. It is likely that every donor and specialized agency, with its own mandates and policy preferences, will propose ambitious projects for creating or re-creating Cambodian entities capable of working in each respective area or discipline. An excess of such efforts can only weaken the effectiveness of such institution building and lead to frustration.

There is no easy answer to this latter problem. Any one person's or planning unit's agenda of institutional priorities is likely to be criticized by others as blind to the importance of things accorded lower priority or put off to later years. Unfortunately, despite all the accumulated experience and literature on the subject of institution building in developing countries, there is virtually no guidance available on institutional development as a gradual networking process, taking into account such factors as resource endowment, economic size and structure, and the international availability and cost of acquiring specific capabilities from outside as compared with, in effect, intellectual import-substitution. If some rationalizing criteria for choice among institution-building alternatives could be developed, Cambodia in the 1990s will be a country where such criteria could be of very great use, especially for the aid agencies that will be major participants and financiers in Cambodian human resource development.

An example of a priority in time is suggested by this discussion of institutional capacity building. Improvements in public sector capacity and efficiency across the board, in the existing institutional structure, could be designed and installed by a central unit (perhaps attached to the budget function) for organization and management. Such a unit would have to rely on technical assistance for its startup work and for its own establishment, but might become relatively self-reliant in five to seven years. All aid-financed programs might benefit from the work of such a unit, as would public sector institution-building projects down the road.

The prestige and policy influence of senior administrators should be bolstered by the external agencies. In none of the other countries referred to above has the technocratic class had an independent power base. They have sustained their hold on policy formation through competence, alliances of convenience with the holders of military and political power, and backing from international donors and agencies. In the case of Cambodia, however, the international agencies will have a presence more penetrating into the normal business of government than is usually the case. While this influence will give the agencies unusual scope in training Cambodian counterparts and strengthening their prestige, there is always a danger that too overt or heavy-handed foreign support of these counterparts could undermine their credibility and open them to charges of being foreign tools. The support role is vital, but delicate.

It is unlikely that the deficit in top administrative capacity can be much reduced through recruitment of people among the returnees from the border camps. In some skills (e.g., English language interpreters, health workers) the returnees include many qualified people who will be an important addition to Cambodia's human resources. But few will have qualifications for national-level policy and management, at least immediately. Short-course in-service training will be important for strengthening administrative capacities without robbing ongoing activities of experienced personnel.

Two other options for quickly strengthening senior administration have begun to be explored. One is to draw on the overseas Cambodian communities, briefly discussed below. The second is to provide resident advisers through the normal channels of international technical assistance. The arrangements for the core policy management functions will be particularly important. These include revenue and budget, statistics and economic monitoring, the central bank, aid coordination, major sector policy orientation (industry, trade, etc.), legislative drafting, and so on.

It would be desirable for advisers for such core functions to be accepted by the Cambodian authorities as, in effect, members of their civil service, as temporary Cambodians dedicated to strengthening Cambodian governance and administration immediately, and to helping the authorities cope with external agencies and negotiations. Constituted as a team, the group could also serve the important role of helping to integrate the workings of their respective departments into their complementary functions as they relate to cross-cutting policies and programs. Close professional association between the members of the team and their Cambodian counterparts would be tantamount to an extended on-the-job orientation into the accumulated experience of development management from which Cambodia has been isolated for so long.

All of this puts a heavy responsibility on the international agencies and donors. With all due respect to the need to sustain Cambodian sovereignty (as reflected in the Agreements language that puts off definition of *development* policy until a postelection government is in position to define it), the outsiders will be operating in what amounts to a policy vacuum in the short run, and for some time will be in the position de facto of shaping policies. Regardless of UNTAC's fate, aid resources are likely to be so large in relation to government revenue, and agency technical assistance so great in relation to the local bureaucracy, that the outsiders will have substantial influence. It is vital that this role be played with a coherence beneficial to the country's redevelopment.

The Human Condition

The measures central to the World Bank program, and the inevitable focus of a large fraction of the early rehabilitation and development expenditures, address the problems of macroeconomic stability and of the financial requirements for restoring essential infrastructure to working order. While these activities are indeed necessary, they will provide only a framework (albeit a positive one) for what happens, or fails to happen, that will determine whether or not Cambodia's villagers settle into social stability, resistant to purveyors of divisiveness, conspiracy theories, and racial hatreds and upheaval. The progress of the human condition, even in the short run, is closely tied to the achievement of the political desideratum of the entire UN effort. This is evidently recognized by the Khmer Rouge, who have taken every opportunity to try to block UNTAC's effort to restore essential services, principally the rural health and education systems.

As described by the World Bank, the sketchy data available paint "an extremely bleak picture of adverse social conditions caused by poverty, war, meager health care, and very poor household hygiene." Malaria, dengue fever, tuberculosis, intestinal and respiratory infections, and micronutrient deficiencies affect very large numbers of the population. Malnutrition is estimated to affect 20 percent of the provincial population. Life expectancy is less than fifty years. Infant and maternal mortality rates are among the highest in the world. Less than 15 percent of the rural population has access to safe drinking water. An estimated three hundred fifty thousand inhabitants have been disabled by stepping on mines, giving Cambodia the highest rate of physically disabled people in the world. More are being disabled every day. There is a very limited capability for fitting child amputees with prostheses.

One of the most important problems bearing on village health, agriculture, and other activities is demographic: male casualties of the past two decades have been much greater than female. As a result, an estimated 70 percent of the rural labor force is female. Roughly one-third of all households are headed by women, mostly widows. While the economic position of widows who have male children can be expected to improve over time as the children grow into their teens, there are large numbers who, at present and for some years to come, appear to be among the most disadvantaged in Cambodia, apart from unskilled amputees.

Studies of Cambodian refugees in the United States and in the border camps[8] have shown a high incidence of mental health problems among adult women as a consequence of their traumatic experiences under the Khmer Rouge and the subsequent dislocations. Some observers argue that those who remained in the country and returned to their home villages are likely to have suffered less trauma than those who have lived in the camps or who have had to adjust to new cultures in the United States and elsewhere. While there have been no comparable studies conducted in Cambodia, knowledgeable observers report the presence of similar psychosomatic symptoms[9] that could well be contributing to the disadvantaged position of Cambodian women and widow-headed households. Just how disadvantaged these households are is not well known and depends on the members' general health, the number of dependent children, the amount and quality of land they received in the privatization of the agriculture collectives, whether or not they own buffalo or other productive assets, etc. The point that is now generally accepted—that gender division of agricultural work must be taken into account in agricultural development programs in all developing countries—applies with special force to Cambodia. Much more must be learned about these households and the knowledge fed into the standard sectoral work.

The ways in which village communities function and respond to outside interventions, however benign, will be critical to the feasibility of many programs: community-based primary health care, water-user farm cooperation in irrigation systems, credit guarantee grouping as a basis for small farmer credit, use of progressive farmers as entry points for adoption of new farming methods, food for work programs requiring community participation on local public works projects, self-help organizations for mobilizing village resources, and so on. The United Nations Children's Fund (UNICEF) has probably acquired more field experience than other agencies thus far in the operation of programs dependent on village and family-level dynamics, but this experience (and the experience of nongovernmental organizations conducting similar projects) has been on a relatively small scale and has not yet been evaluated in sufficient depth.

All programs dependent on the response of rural families and communities suffer from a dearth of research into Cambodian family and community dynamics. The handful of students who have carried out village studies in Cambodia, almost all foreigners, did their work in the 1960s. Systematic social study has barely revived, and the few individuals (Khmer and foreign) who have developed more recent insights are stressing the profound changes (largely deleterious) they detect in interpersonal relations and community dynamics as a result of the trauma and dislocation of the past twenty years.

A program of social research in Cambodia should quickly be

initiated. A few individuals and graduate students have managed to undertake systematic study involving field research. With the revival in recent years of academic interest in Southeast Asia, a program oriented to field research would probably attract many students of anthropology, political science, and other disciplines. Operational agencies have a direct interest in fostering such research. UNICEF's village programs (like the Family Food Production project, in cooperation with local authorities and the SOC's Women's Association), for example, make implicit assumptions about the situation and response of widow-headed families that need to be tested and professionally monitored. Production outcomes are easily observed. But the presumed effects on empowerment, on permanence of changes in the economic position and options of these families, are still matters of speculation.

While foreign researchers will have to undertake the bulk of social science field study in Cambodia for several years, research capability must be developed in local academic institutions. Precisely where such capabilities should be located, what disciplines should be involved, scale and degrees to be offered, etc., are questions for a major institution-building effort.

Another perspective concerns replicability and the pace of "scaling up." The extent to which health, educational, agricultural, and other systems and programs can be extended in geographic and population coverage over the next decade, and strengthened in content and quality, depends to some degree (political stability aside) on the general issues already touched upon (budget recovery, senior management capabilities, field research and evaluation, etc.).

But some observers believe that Cambodian society underneath has been very "loosely structured." They detect little tendency to form interest groups or other kinds of organizations outside the family. In Cambodia today village authorities are appointed by the government, and the few mass movements (e.g., the Women's Association) have been created by the SOC originally as instruments of political mobilization. The apparent disinterest in spontaneously organizing communal activities has been reinforced, according to some observers, by the effects on individual behavior of the traumas suffered under the Khmer Rouge. Fear of unpredictable consequences, uncertainty over who can be trusted, a traumatically engraved passivity as the primary survival skill under a regime in which safety depended on not being noticed, even a kind of internal blankness as a substrate for external passivity—these and other reactions and symptoms of an isolating and depressing character have been assumed to be operating to reinforce the traditional atomistic mores. Even if such psychological factors are indeed affecting behavior, they may be less inhibiting respecting activities internal to the individual village community than to association with outside structures.

These yet poorly understood factors reinforce the importance of undertaking a search for decentralized organizational alternatives, given the prospect that the effective programmatic outreach of central government will remain very weak for some time to come. Under these conditions, it is surprising that the external agencies and foreign nongovernmental organizations (NGOs) have not paid more attention to the one traditional, indigenous, independent institution found at the village level as an exception to the lack of social structures—the Buddhist temple. While the Buddhist monkhood and hierarchy bears little resemblance to the highly structured and disciplined organization of, say, the Catholic church, the village temple has long been the center of communal life in Cambodia. The village monks have carried on ceremonial life and have taught the Cambodian worldview from one generation to the next. After the decimation by the Khmer Rouge, and the limits placed on entry into the monkhood by the SOC until rather recently, there has been a strong revival at the village level. Particularly striking has been the willingness of villagers to donate scarce resources to refurbishing the temples.

Apparently, large numbers of the monks are young new entrants with limited Buddhist education. The monkhood's large training needs raise the possibility of introducing new secular skills that would enable the temples to serve as centers of local, self-help development activities. In Thailand the training of monks for village self-help development activities has been well established for many years, including training in the relevant secular subjects at the Buddhist University in Bangkok. One Khmer monastery in northeast Thailand is already providing similar training, along with education in Buddhism, to young monks from the border camps. The application of this model to Cambodia could well be the most transferable, workable option available in the search for community modalities that would not be artificial implants.

[Margin note: This has not worked well in the cases I know of. The monks became politicized!]

Foreign NGOs have made important contributions in Cambodia to help extend the administration's reach in health, education, and child-welfare services.[10] Thus far the one Khmer NGO that has been established is the work of a Cambodian woman who has returned after having lived and been educated abroad.

Some of the international NGOs have had good experience elsewhere fostering the development of indigenous chapters or independent local organizations. They should be encouraged (and financed) to make similar efforts in Cambodia. Of course, successor Cambodian governments may be wary of domestic NGOs, apprehensive over their possible development as political instruments. Experience elsewhere has shown that NGOs, especially when numerous enough to form associations, can serve as entry points for the practice of what are, in effect, pluralistic politics, even though their work is not actually political per se. Their work can be a positive contribution in a society with little history of political pluralism. While the SOC has had very positive experience with the international NGOs (virtually the only windows to the West until recently), domestic counterparts that are not creatures of government may look like an entirely different animal.

The transition to a market economy should generate profit-driven activity with potentially much greater reach and economic impact than can be obtained through bureaucratically administered activity. The development of new irrigation systems, research and extension services, and other standard government programs, which will certainly have a role in Cambodia over time, tend to take many years to raise farm income. In the meantime there may be opportunities to encourage the development of private agribusiness that can help raise farm income (e.g., through contract farming) without heavy reliance on administered systems.

An area of special interest is nonfarm income opportunities for women. It is known that in Cambodia rural families earn a substantial fraction of their annual income from off-farm and/or nonagricultural activities in the off-season. Several constraints have been identified as barriers to keeping these nonfarm activities from becoming dynamic sources of income growth: lack of credit, inadequate skills, absence of marketing networks, and heavy claims on women's time regardless of the agriculture season. A few ad hoc attempts are being made to loosen these constraints, mostly small-scale projects assisted by UNICEF and a few NGOs. These projects have had mixed results. Those that appear to be unsuccessful (that is, not viable for scaling up as free-standing, profitable activities) suffer from the difficulty of overcoming all the relevant constraints within the administered framework (even with management-intensive oversight) that characterizes their conception.

Here again alternative private sector, commercial solutions should be sought. While female employment can be expected to rise if Cambodia is able to turn its relatively low wages to advantage as the basis for an export-oriented industrial strategy, generating employment for rural female heads of households presents problems that warrant special approaches.

Textile production is typically a large employer of female labor. Silk is a particularly interesting product because of the possibilities it offers for a putting-out system that can accommodate the time allocation patterns of village women. The model that might be adapted to Cambodian conditions is the early period of commercialization of Thai silk-weaving by Jim Thompson in the 1940s and 1950s. As with the contract farming model, the Thompson organization provided the inputs, technical and design oversight, and marketing, building this female employment engine into a major export industry. As a private venture, it could not afford to rely on government inputs, in effect economizing on what was then, in Thailand, a scarce management resource.

The Thai Khmer

The need to develop basic knowledge of the dynamics of community and family life, as a key element in the development of workable rural programs, points to the potential parallels and lessons that might be gleaned from the ethnic Khmer in northeast Thailand. There are roughly eight hundred fifty thousand ethnic Khmer in Thailand. Unlike the Cambodian refugees, these largely rural Khmer are Thai citizens living in an area that has had a Khmer population for centuries. In contrast with the experience of the Khmer inside Cambodia, the Thai Khmer have lived in a relatively stable social environment and have been integrated into the primary health, education, and other development programs and safety nets (as well as the transportation and private sector activities) that have been part of Thailand's rural evolution. Thus the Thai Khmer may serve as a natural experiment. The extent to which parallels may be drawn, the degrees of similarity in worldview and social dynamics, are matters that would need some investigation to ensure that no facile or misleading conclusions are drawn as to what might work well in Cambodia. Nevertheless, an examination of the recent development of Khmer villages in Thailand, and the workings of health and other programs, could be more illuminating than lessons that have been drawn from the operations of such programs in other countries.

The Khmer population of Thailand could also be a source of expertise that would have comparative advantages over technical personnel from somewhere else. Khmer professionals in Thailand would have obvious language and cultural affinities other foreign professionals would lack. They might also have relevant experience of a kind probably not available in either the border camp populations or the Khmer communities in the United States, France, and elsewhere. An effort should be made to explore these potentialities.

The Cambodian Expatriate Communities

There has been a lot of speculation as to the contributions the expatriate Cambodian communities might make to the country's reconstruction. The expatriates number about two hundred fifty thousand and are settled mainly in the United States (one hundred seventy-five thousand), France (forty thousand), Canada (thirteen thousand), Australia (thirteen thousand), and New Zealand and Switzerland. The main contribution thus far has come in the form of individual remittances to family members still living in Cambodia. Information on remittances is incomplete, since only a portion has been transmitted through formal bank transfers. The lifting of the U.S. embargo on Cambodia (announced on January 4, 1992) should open the door to a substantial increase. Remittances already may be larger than Cambodia's recorded export earnings and, along with UNTAC expenditures and the resumption of economic aid should be an important source of income growth in the next few years. Remittances benefit directly those Cambodians who happen to have overseas relatives (and then indirectly, of course, those who provide the goods and services on which this income is spent). As welcome as remittances will be for the country's recovery, it must be noted that this inflow, as long as it remains largely family by family, is likely to create a sharp economic differentiation between the direct recipients and the rest of the population. At current income levels in Cambodia, a family remittance of, for example, $400 to $500 a year would create a major income differential between recipients and their nonrecipient neighbors or covillagers.

Given the importance of the remittances, this subject should be explored in future economic analyses. Are the recipient relatives largely urban dwellers, or is the income spreading beyond Phnom Penh and a few large towns? What can be done to encourage a larger inflow, especially by institutions that can mobilize such funds for programs of welfare and economic development that are, as yet, underfunded. There are some organized private aid activities already under way, but the potential for this type of assistance from Khmer communities overseas appears relatively untapped thus far. This is an area in which NGOs could take some initiatives.

Other roles for the overseas communities are being launched or considered: private investment, NGOs, advisory positions for Cambodian academics and professionals working for international and other agencies, technical assistance through international development agencies, etc. With their advantages of language and cultural understanding, expatriates in such roles could make important contributions toward easing the constraints on absorptive capacity and facilitating the management and expansion of programs being assisted by international agencies. The main questions and hurdles that would have to be addressed to develop these roles have become readily apparent as the expatriates themselves have begun to discuss the possibilities and to visit Cambodia.

UNTAC and External Agencies

The international aid and peacekeeping activities, and the follow-on donor development programs, should be looked at as an economic sector that will pump up general purchasing power and stimulate demand for specific goods and services. Urban housing and office space, urban utilities, fresh foods, local employment (translators, drivers, office workers, domestics, miscellaneous maintenance and services, etc.), small-scale construction contracting and materials, tourism, restaurants, and entertainment services are among the goods and services the international community is acquiring from the local economy and inflating in price. The macroeconomic and price implications of the activities of this sector in the period leading up to the elections are being monitored and, hopefully, addressed by UNTAC and the relevant international agencies. But the activities of this sector, quite apart from the rehabilitation projects, should also be looked at from a perspective of long-term impact.

Attention needs to be given to possible distortions and undesirable effects. Local procurement and hiring will undoubtedly concentrate in Phnom Penh. Given the recent disastrous consequences of urban-rural division in Cambodian society, the international community should seek to deconcentrate its activities and procurement wherever possible, consistent of course with each agency's primary responsibilities. Large distortions in the local wage structure might be avoided through coordination of wage scales, establishment of a central information clearinghouse on skilled manpower requirements, and avoidance of raiding and pyramiding competition for skill categories that can be increased only slowly in the short run. An interesting example of a possible positive spinoff is the suggestion (developed by a consultant to the CARE office in Phnom Penh) that the international community residing in Cambodia adopt a policy of favoring the employment of amputees. To supply suitably skilled amputees (fitted with prostheses) to meet such affirmative action demand, a special training program would have to be developed.

As a major employer and contractor, the international sector should also avoid contributing to ethnic divisions in the marketplace. It was commonly said in 1991, even before UNTAC had arrived on the scene, that the construction workers on the many villas being refurbished in Phnom Penh were Vietnamese. While the past ethnic divisions of economic roles are not all being re-created (e.g., rubber plantation workers, Vietnamese in the past, are now Khmer), there is enough conspicuous division in Phnom Penh to feed Cambodian antipathy toward ethnic Vietnamese. Recent press reports speak of a resurgence of violence and hatred against local Vietnamese.[11] Given the large numbers of Vietnamese who have reportedly returned to live in Cambodia since the pogroms of the Lon Nol and Khmer Rouge regimes, these antipathies pose extraordinarily difficult problems for UNTAC.

The resurgence has arisen from the propaganda of the Khmer Rouge and other non-SOC factions seeking to exploit the identification of the Hun Sen government as a client of Vietnam. The immediate challenge to UNTAC relates to its responsibilities for law and order and to determining eligibility for registration for the vote. It would be a sad irony if UNTAC managed to contain these problems enough to hold the elections, while at the same time contributed to the reopening of old ethnic and other social and economic fault lines, and then packed its bags, leaving behind a society threatened by rising structural tensions. It may be unrealistic to call on UNTAC's administrators, charged with enormously difficult time-bound tasks, to fine-tune their activities at the same time in order, in effect, to save the Cambodians from themselves. An early reassessment of the UN's role in Cambodia, looking beyond the Agreements as now formulated and defining an extended presence, might enable UNTAC to adjust its intellectual frame of reference and undertake the luxury of thinking about its role in a longer-term and historical context.

There is no denying that Cambodia's geopolitical importance in the aftermath of the cold war has declined. In this context, the interest of the outside world and the unprecedented opportunity the UNTAC experiment offers to the Cambodian people might go either way, continuing in a peacekeeping and society-healing transition or packing up to complete a process of the outside world washing its hands of intractable problems. Cambodia as victim now commands world sympathy that can sustain substantial interest and assistance. Perhaps the most important advice for Prince Sihanouk and the non-Khmer Rouge factions is to work hard against any fanning of traditional hatreds. Cambodia as tormentor of the non-Khmer could quickly erode that sympathy and destroy the experiment.

Notes

1. The basic Agreements on a Comprehensive Political Settlement of the Cambodia Conflict submitted to the UN by the French and Indonesian copresidents of the Paris International Conference on Cambodia are contained in UN document General Assembly/Security Council, A/46/608, S/23177, 30 October 1991.

2. For a full account of Khmer Rouge (newly self-styled as the Party of Democratic Kampuchea) violation of the Agreements, see "Special Report of the Secretary-General on the United Nations Transitional Authority in Cambodia," Security Council, S/24090, 12 June 1992.

3. David A. Abling and Marlowe Hood, eds., *The Cambodian Agony* (Armonk, N.Y.: M. E. Sharpe, 1987): xix.

4. Serge Thion, "The Pattern of Cambodian Politics," in *The Cambodian Agony,* ed. David A. Abling and Marlowe Hood (Armonk, N.Y.: M. E. Sharpe, 1987): 162.

5. David P. Chandler, *The Tragedy of Cambodian History* (New Haven, Conn.: Yale University Press, 1991): 316-17.

6. The World Bank, *Cambodia: Agenda for Rehabilitation and Reconstruction* (June 1992).

7. Ibid., iii.

8. See *Repatriation and Disability: A Community Study of Health, Mental Health and Social Functioning of the Khmer Residents of Site Two,* published by Harvard School of Public Health and the World Federation for Mental Health (1992), and the bibliography therein.

9. See, for example, May Ebihara, "Beyond Suffering: The Recent History of a Cambodian Village," in *The Challenge of Economic Reform in Indochina,* ed. B. Ljundggren and P. Timmer (Cambridge, Mass.: Harvard Institute for International Development/Harvard University Press, forthcoming).

10. Brief descriptions of nongovernmental organization activities are given in *Humanitarian Assistance in Cambodia,* published annually by the NGO Forum and available from the U.S.-Indochina Reconciliation Project, New York.

11. *Far East Economic Review,* 30 July 1992.

III

Human Rights in Cambodia: Past, Present, and Future

Sidney Jones and Dinah PoKempner

The very word *Cambodia* conjures up an image of one of the worst human rights disasters of the century. Because of the horrors of Khmer Rouge rule between 1975 and 1979, protection of human rights in Cambodia is often seen as synonymous with preventing the Khmer Rouge from returning to power, through military force or as part of a transitional government. But the problem is far more complex, involving nothing less than a fundamental alteration in how the state treats its citizens; the unification of a deeply divided society; the balance between the legitimate security concerns of a country in chaos and the need to create political space; and the protection of particularly vulnerable groups of people, including returning refugees and ethnic Vietnamese.

Following is a brief look at the past, present, and future of human rights protection in Cambodia, with specific attention to the rights guaranteed under the International Covenant on Civil and Political Rights, an international treaty to which the Supreme National Council (SNC) in Cambodia has acceded and all four parties represented on the SNC—the State of Cambodia (SOC); Democratic Kampuchea (the Khmer Rouge); the National United Front for an Independent, Neutral, Peaceful and Cooperative Cambodia (FUNCINPEC), loyal to Prince Sihanouk; and the Khmer People's National Liberation Front (KPNLF), nominally led by former prime minister Son Sann—have agreed to accept. Those rights include the right not to be arbitrarily deprived of life; the right not to be subjected to cruel, inhuman, or degrading treatment or punishment;

freedom from arbitrary arrest or detention; freedom of movement and choice of residence; the right to a fair trial; freedom of thought, conscience, and religion; and the freedoms of expression, association, and assembly.

Until a new government is elected, the United Nations Transitional Authority in Cambodia (UNTAC) is responsible for guaranteeing the protection of these rights by investigating complaints and taking "corrective action" wherever necessary. It is also responsible for laying the groundwork for a "neutral political environment conducive to free and fair elections," meaning that it can remove officials, revoke laws, control the civilian police, and override any administrative actions that work against the objectives of the Paris Agreements. UNTAC is in effect charged with creating a functioning civil society in Cambodia, where there has never been one before.

The Past

The tendency to focus on the brutality of the Khmer Rouge obscures the fact that Cambodians have never been protected from the arbitrary use of executive authority.

Prince Norodom Sihanouk himself was no champion of civil liberties. On the contrary, he personified arbitrary rule. In the 1950s he frequently arrested and charged political opponents with treason for having the effrontery to question his policies. From 1955 on, political parties, for all practical purposes, ceased to function. On one notorious occasion, in August 1957, he invited members of the opposition Democratic Party to debate him, ensuring their presence by sending police agents to their homes and warning it would be considered treasonous if they failed to show up. When they did, he harangued them for three hours and sent them home. As they left the palace grounds, Sihanouk's palace guard pulled them from their cars and savagely beat them with rifle butts.[1] In the period 1963-70, Sihanouk sanctioned a program of state-sponsored terror against suspected leftists, involving widespread arrests and executions and compelling hundreds of Cambodian students and professionals to join the guerrillas of the Communist Party of Kampuchea in the jungle:

> Many survivors of the 1960s have recalled an atmosphere of terror that pervaded intellectual circles and smothered student politics in Phnom Penh. . . . As government-sponsored violence became widespread and remained unpunished, the fabric of Cambodian self-confidence, never tightly woven, began to unravel. A former schoolteacher has recalled that several of his colleagues were held without charges in the late 1960s, while others disappeared—either into the maquis or killed by the police. In some regions rewards were given for rebels' severed heads. In Kampot in 1969, several alleged dissidents were thrown alive off a high cliff; their heads were later displayed in the Kampot market.[2]

General Lon Nol's rule from 1970 to 1975 was hardly an improvement. In May 1970, a month after he took power in a coup, his soldiers and police massacred thousands of ethnic Vietnamese men, women, and children in and around Phnom Penh, apparently on the assumption that they must be Viet Cong sympathizers. As one observer believes, "At best the killings showed that Lon Nol was unable to control the violence of his subordinates; at worst, they revealed that Lon Nol and his associates were willing to conduct a racially based religious war against unarmed civilians whose families had lived in Cambodia for generations."[3] Political detentions and disappearances were commonplace, and increased as the security situation in Cambodia deteriorated. Atrocities by soldiers of the Khmer Republic, such as slicing open the bodies of captured Khmer Rouge soldiers and eating the liver, were routine.[4] Elections in 1972 were blatantly rigged, and corruption was rampant.

Thus, even before the Khmer Rouge marched into Phnom Penh in April 1975, Cambodians had no experience with an open society, and they have had none since, either in the People's Republic of Kampuchea (PRK)—turned State of Cambodia in 1989—or in the camps along the Thai-Cambodian border.

The question of human rights in the PRK/SOC has been hotly debated. Some observers have seen the government of Heng Samrin, Hun Sen, and Chea Sim primarily as a Khmer government aided by Vietnam, which did a reasonable job of trying to impose some kind of order on a country decimated and devastated by almost four years of Khmer Rouge rule. Others have seen it as a Vietnamese-installed government composed of ex-Khmer Rouge members in which the party dominated all and basic civil liberties were nil.[5] It is beyond dispute that the Khmer Rouge left behind a country with virtually all civil institutions destroyed; it would be difficult to protect human rights under the best of circumstances with no courts, no laws, and almost no lawyers. On the other hand, throughout the 1980s there were widespread reports of torture and inhumane conditions in PRK prisons, inexcusable under any circumstances, and the International Committee of the Red Cross was not allowed into those prisons on its own terms until early 1992, well after the October 1991 release of some 442 political prisoners and 483 "prisoners of war."[6]

Freedom of expression was also absent in the PRK/SOC until 1992. In May 1990 a group of intellectuals and senior officials led by former minister of transportation Ung Phan tried to test the political waters by organizing an independent political group, the Liberal Social Democratic Party. Everyone involved was arrested and detained until just before the Paris Agreements were signed on October 23, 1991. As the indefinite detention of political opponents became a more difficult option for the State of Cambodia after the Paris accords, other means of depriving citizens of basic rights became more visible: legislative or administrative regulation of expression and association; maintenance of political dossiers on citizens; restrictions on freedom of movement; threats against former political prisoners to intimidate them into refraining from political activity; and physical attacks on opponents by often unidentified assailants.

Some of those who had castigated the PRK for denial of human rights held up the noncommunist resistance as a paragon of democratic virtue, but the camps along the Thai-Cambodian border run by the two noncommunist factions afforded the Cambodians who lived there little freedom. Whether run by the KPNLF, FUNCINPEC, or Khmer Rouge, the camps, where three hundred sixty thousand Cambodians have lived for much of the last thirteen years have each been controlled by one faction, and justice has been traditionally dispensed by military strongmen acting through camp administrators. The fact that those strongmen for the most part emerged from the army or police active under Sihanouk, Lon Nol, or Pol Pot says a good deal about their knowledge of or respect for human rights. (Son Sann, nominal head of the KPNLF, is a man of unquestioned integrity; he also has almost no control over different factions of the KPNLF and their military forces.)

Each of the factions has a long and unenviable record of human rights abuse in the camps. Coerced military service, forced portering across the border into Cambodia, and officially sanctioned or tolerated attacks and killings have been common. In early 1987, in response to sharply escalating violence in the camps, the United Nations Border Relief Operation (UNBRO) instituted a "protection unit." Despite the widely held assumption that only a fraction of incidents ever reached UNBRO's attention, an astonishing number of complaints were recorded in the first two years, including 792 incidents of beating, 261 incidents of knifing or axing, 101 shootings, 57 assaults by shelling or mines, 52 assaults by grenade, 64 rapes or other forms of sexual abuse, and 164 suicides.[7] Despite such violence, it was virtually impossible to request a transfer from one camp ruled by one faction to another.

In an attempt to grapple with the problem of official complicity in extortion, rape, assault, and murder, UNBRO developed a code of justice, prison rules, and informal courts called justice committees. The latter was first instituted at the largest KPNLF camp, Site 2, in May 1989. The success of these committees may be judged by one case brought to trial in May 1992 in which the defendant was none other than the chief judge of the Site 2 justice committee, who was accused of raping the seventeen-year-old sister of his fourth wife. Before his arrest the defendant had sent soldiers to threaten the deputy judge trying the case and threatened to kill his accuser if she proceeded with the charges. His supporters placed land mines in front of the prosecutor's house, and even after a sentence of four and a half years in prison was handed down, the accused continued to threaten vengeance. The case was highly unusual only in that the charges stuck.

If violence and corruption in Site 2 have been endemic over the years, they have been worse in Site B, a Sihanoukist camp, run on an almost feudal system of allegiance to Prince Sihanouk and his son, Prince Ranariddh, the current head of the FUNCINPEC. Boys under the age of fifteen are pressured to work for the military, and in contrast to Site 8, the most open of Khmer Rouge camps, there have been no free elections for section leaders (administrative divisions within the camp). Instead administrators practice what they call "directed democracy."

Abuses in the Khmer Rouge camps have been well documented, ranging from execution and forced portering to conscription of children and denial of food and medical care.[8] The fact that the Khmer Rouge camps have in general been less subject to random violence than the noncommunist camps may reflect a higher degree of control and fear than exists in the latter. Two weeks before the Paris Agreements were signed, the Khmer Rouge apparently was on the verge of sending all forty thousand residents of Site 8 back into Cambodia. On September 30, 1991, the party detained sixteen elected administrators of Site 8 and appointed new, reportedly more hardline, officials to take their place. The sixteen were called to report to a meeting in the Khmer Rouge military base at Phnom Dey, inside Cambodia. The UN and Prince Sihanouk made strong protests to the Khmer Rouge, who ultimately let the Site 8 residents remain in the camp, but concentrations of Khmer Rouge soldiers remained, visiting residents at night and attempting to intimidate them into returning to Khmer Rouge-held territory.[9]

In short, neither Cambodians who survived the Khmer Rouge era nor those who fled to the border camps, who together will constitute the citizenry of the post-UNTAC Cambodia and from whom the future leadership will be drawn, have direct experience in having or responsibly exercising fundamental human rights.

The Present

Given that lack of experience, the magnitude of what has to happen before human rights can be protected becomes apparent. With UNTAC playing a major role, freedom of access into and out of all parts of Cambodia must be secured; politically neutral institutions have to be established; tolerance for different political views has to be learned and practiced by all sides; racial invective against the ethnic Vietnamese must cease; and workable mechanisms for registering complaints of human rights abuse and enforcing compliance with human rights standards must be put in place.

All of this must take place in a country still divided between a government in Phnom Penh that controls about 80 percent of the country; zones controlled by the FUNCINPEC, KPNLF, and Khmer Rouge near the Thai border; an unknown number of villages nominally under SOC, KPNLF, or FUNCINPEC control but heavily infiltrated by the Khmer Rouge; and the hundreds of thousands of Cambodians anxious to return from the Thai camps. As the elections are scheduled for May 1993, it is in the interests of each party to retain control over as many people as possible, and some of the ongoing human rights abuses stem from the efforts of the three former resistance factions to thwart or wrest control of the repatriation process so as to ensure that as many people as possible move to the zones.

Above and beyond the difficulties of establishing this human rights infrastructure, the peace process itself becomes a complicating factor. A return to full-scale civil war would undoubtedly result in a drastic escalation of human rights abuses, so it is clearly in the interest of human rights protection to keep the peace process on track. At the same time, bending over backwards to avoid offending any one of the four parties in the interest of moving forward on the implementation of the accords can set a dangerous precedent for toleration of abuses. The dilemma is most obvious with respect to the Khmer Rouge. When does the international community call a halt to Khmer Rouge noncompliance, and what does it do to end political infiltration of Cambodian villages and reassertion of Khmer Rouge control there?

Freedom of Movement. Two essential aspects of human rights protection in the transitional period (if indeed implementation of the accords stays on course) are access by all parties including UNTAC personnel to all areas of the country and freedom of all Cambodians to move out from under the control of repressive officials. The fact that the access to Khmer Rouge areas remains all but impossible, even for the head of UNTAC, Yasushi Akashi, suggests both that human rights violations continue in these areas and that the Khmer Rouge leadership fears that increased access would weaken its control.

It is ironic that as of September 1992 the Phnom Penh government had been the target of most of the human rights complaints received by UNTAC's human rights component, in part because the UN and other foreign observers had better access to SOC territory than to territory controlled by the other three factions and more opportunity to disseminate information about its work. The access also means that UNTAC can expose abuses and deter future abuses, if it has the will to do so. Since, however, the SOC has been the most cooperative of the factions and since its cooperation is critical to the success of the UN mission, UNTAC has been reluctant to embarrass Phnom Penh officials by public reporting of complaints—another example of the dilemma of balancing peacekeeping and human rights protection.

Establishment of Politically Neutral Institutions. Removing key institutions from the control of one faction is essential to the creation of a politically neutral atmosphere. As far as human rights protection is concerned, the most important of these institutions to be neutralized are the armed forces, the police, and the courts. The disarming and cantonment of 70 percent of each faction's armed forces, provided for in the Paris Agreements, had stalled in late 1992 because of Khmer Rouge obstructionism, and military leaders still controlled the zones.

The police forces under the accords were to be supervised but not disbanded by UNTAC. According to UNTAC, as of late 1992 the SOC had forty-seven thousand police, the Khmer Rouge nine thousand, the FUNCINPEC one hundred fifty, and the KPNLF none. The dominance of the SOC was at once disturbing, despite the latter's relatively good cooperation with UNTAC and the fact that over two thousand UNTAC police supervisors were already deployed as of September 1992 in all twenty one provinces down to the district level. But in any country in which arbitrary detention of political dissidents has been a major problem, the power of arrest becomes critical. The SOC's Ministry of the Interior, which until April 1992 controlled both ordinary police and the notorious A-3 unit (which among other things was involved in military recruitment along the Thai-Cambodian border), was known as the bastion of hardline Marxist orthodoxy. In April responsibility for both police and prisons was placed under a newly created Ministry for National Security, and the UN began training sessions to introduce police to the UN code of conduct for law enforcement officials, which among other things stresses the need to apply the principle of proportionality in the use of lethal force. But as of September 1992, UNTAC had made little, if any progress in disbanding SOC internal security agencies and several clandestine detention centers had been uncovered.

There is little for UNTAC to supervise in the justice system. Between six and ten professionally educated lawyers remained in the country after the Khmer Rouge killings, and their number has declined as a few have died since 1979. The Phnom Penh government has created courts in each of the country's eighteen provinces and two municipalities, but judges have only rudimentary training and handle relatively few cases. There is no pretense of judicial independence, and the Ministry of the Interior has generally refused to cooperate with efforts of public prosecutors and judges to enforce legal restraints on the arbitrary detention of suspects or maltreatment of prisoners.[10] As of late 1992 UNTAC was about to introduce a new penal code, and in the area of criminal law was giving priority detention of suspects, and proportionality between crimes and punishments.

If courts were weak in areas controlled by the SOC, they were utterly lacking in the zones. Serious offenders were brought before military administrators for judgment. Neither the code of justice nor the justice committees that had been operative, imperfectly, in the camps were used in the zones. The two noncommunist factions claim they hold few prisoners in their territories, but reports suggest that prisoners may be summarily executed rather than held. (In December 1991 two KPNLF soldiers wanted for crimes were handed over to the KPNLF military by police in Site 2; they were taken to Svay Chek, in KPNLF-held territory inside Cambodia, and shot "while trying to escape.")

The lack of checks on military authority in the zones makes efforts by the KPNLF, FUNCINPEC, and Khmer Rouge to force or encourage repatriation there all the more disturbing. Each resistance faction has waged a campaign to persuade refugees to return to the zones. The campaigns tend to play on the fear of persecution or attack in SOC territory and the purported inability of the UN to protect or provide adequate land and assistance for those who repatriate under UN auspices. The aim is clearly to try to retain control over camp residents even as they leave the camps, since each faction, including the Khmer Rouge, sees the key to its political survival in the creation of a firm territorial base before the elections take place. That base will provide an electorate, a labor force with which to continue the lucrative border trade, and a supply of soldiers and porters should fighting resume.

Refugees are subjected to both subtle and overt pressure from different sources to move to the zones. In Site 2 there is rivalry between the various administrations, with different leaders trying to recruit followers and win United Nations High Commissioner for Refugees (UNHCR) assistance in resettling their constituents in areas within the KPNLF zone. In May the KPNLF presented UNHCR with a list of 490 persons who supposedly had houses and land waiting for them in the Thmar Pouk area and who wanted UN transportation to get there as well as rice rations after they arrived.

When UN officials interviewed these people, only 129 were willing to go to the zones under those conditions. Meanwhile, the KPNLF administration in Thmar Pouk has been busy planning settlements for as many as fifty thousand returnees from all camps, including thousands from those controlled by the Khmer Rouge.

The campaigns to move to the zones are bolstered by the deteriorating security situation in the camps. Although military shelling of the camps ended with the cease-fire, a series of natural disasters and bandit attacks have since struck the border population. The attacks appear symptomatic of a general dissolution of the social order in the camps. Many observers also suspect that at least some of the attacks are sanctioned by the factional administrations, in order to increase the likelihood that people, desperate to leave the camps, will repatriate to the zones.

The lack of curbs on military authority in the zones has not prevented the UN from considering them as repatriation sites, especially when by the beginning of 1992 it was clear that there would not be enough safe, accessible land in the northwest provinces to accommodate all refugees who wished to return there. UNHCR began to consider alternative resettlement sites in every area of Cambodia, including the zones. At a January meeting that, among other topics, considered whether and how to assist those persons willing to return to faction-controlled areas, it was agreed that the UN would assist return to those areas under a set of conditions. These conditions included direct and unhindered UNHCR access to the refugees to ascertain the voluntary and free nature of their choice; ascertaining that the areas are safe from the point of view of mines, banditry, and any other relevant security considerations; determining that the areas provide reasonable economic viability; that refugees returning to the zones would briefly pass through reception facilities inside Cambodia; and that there is freedom of movement in and out of the areas, "according to the wishes of the populations."[11]

On May 22, UNHCR transported 436 persons directly from Site 2 to the KPNLF area of Thmar Pouk district, Battambang province, without processing through a reception center in Cambodia. Most of those returned actually had been living in the district, employed in the local administration, education, or health work. More than half had houses of their own, and the remainder were provided shelter by the administration. For this reason UNHCR did not provide the returnees either cash assistance or building materials, much to their disappointment. A second movement of 501 people took place on July 14. Further repatriations are planned for Thmar Pouk and the FUNCINPEC region of Ampil in Banteay Mean Chey province. Prior to departure, UNHCR officials interviewed returnees to ascertain the voluntary nature of their choice.

There are serious questions as to whether conditions in the zones meet all the criteria formulated by UNHCR in January. It is also unclear whether the UN has gained sufficient control over the administration of the zones to monitor adequately the safety and free movement of the populations there, even if a few dozen UNTAC police are now deployed there. The increasing military role of the Khmer Rouge in these areas is especially troubling in this regard. There were reports in late 1992 that the Khmer Rouge was increasingly assuming military control of the zones, especially as the KPNLF and FUNCINPEC militaries disintegrated into small armed gangs. Local administrators reportedly acknowledged and accepted the Khmer Rouge presence, which, they said, was helping to control banditry in the area.

Information on the Khmer Rouge zones themselves is scant but troubling. Most areas are highly malarial, with few medical facilities that are available to civilians. Thousands of residents of the zones travel to Site 8, the Khmer Rouge showcase camp across the border in Thailand, for medical care each year. In contrast to the relative openness of life in Site 8, daily activities are governed closely in the interior, especially near Khmer Rouge base camps, with the party suppressing information from the outside, contact with outsiders, commerce, and religion. Civilians in the interior camps largely subsist on rations handed out by the military, and infractions in discipline are sometimes punished by a cut in rations. Marriage is controlled by the administration, education is nonexistent, and children are enlisted at the earliest age possible.[12] Movement even to a neighboring village in the Khmer Rouge territory requires permission from village and military authorities as to the places and duration of travel. Checkpoints are stationed between every settlement, and one must report to the local authorities to extend a stay. Access in and out of the zone is also tightly controlled.

Toleration of Political Activity. As has been made clear, none of the Cambodian parties to the Paris Agreements has a history of tolerating dissent, and the camps and zones remain under one-party control. A Khmer Rouge diplomat in Phnom Penh told a representative from the human rights organization Asia Watch that dissent was not allowed in areas it administered inside Cambodia. Freedom of expression, he said, would be granted only after UNTAC verified the departure of the Vietnamese.[13]

The SOC, on the other hand, had shown signs of more openness in mid-1992 after an initial spate of attacks on political opponents or critics. By July and August, its efforts to obstruct political organizing by other factions outside Phnom Penh had become a serious problem, and although FUNCINPEC opened an office in Battambang in late September, it remained unclear whether obstructionism would continue.

The period immediately before UNTAC's arrival was marked by a series of attacks on political figures, most notably when, on November 27, 1991, Khmer Rouge leader Khieu Samphan narrowly escaped being lynched by a government-organized mob. It is unclear whether the government anticipated the violent outcome of the demonstration. In denouncing the attack, Prime Minister Hun Sen affirmed for the first time the right of the people to hold nonviolent demonstrations. His position was tested when, on December 17, hundreds of Phnom Penh residents, many of them students, began demonstrations against government corruption. The police response was for the most part restrained until December 21, when two students were beaten and another arrested. When hundreds of students took to the streets to protest and attacked police stations in the process, the police and then soldiers responded by firing on demonstrators. By December 24 eight civilians had died and twenty-six were injured. The government imposed a curfew, banned demonstrations, and subsequently passed legislation allowing the government to ban any demonstration it believes could result in violence.

On January 22, 1992, Tea Bun Long, a government official and member of the FUNCINPEC, was abducted by two men in a jeep and later found shot through the head. He had been an outspoken critic of government corruption. Six days later gunmen shot and wounded Ung Phan, the former transportation minister who had been detained in May 1990 and released in September 1991. He and his fellow detainees had been warned at the time of their release not to engage in political activities, but they nevertheless began reorganizing their political party in December. On January 17, three days after the SNC agreed to accept applications for new political associations, the group announced the formation (or reemergence) of the party, and on January 28 Ung Phan was shot in the neck. The government denied any responsibility for the attack. No suspects have been identified. On March 15 Yang Horn, another former political prisoner linked to Ung Phan, died of a cerebral hemorrhage after an injury to his head caused either by a direct blow or a mysterious fall. No autopsy was performed.

The immediate effect of these attacks was severe intimidation of government critics, but no further murders or attempted murders of major political figures had taken place by September. At the same time, although the KPNLF, FUNCINPEC, and Khmer Rouge set up offices in Phnom Penh, members of these parties were occasionally subjected to attacks and harassment. SOC police attacked KPNLF members in April in different provinces, allegedly because they lacked authorized travel papers. On July 25 they detained KPNLF leader Ieng Mouli, his entourage, and bodyguards as they were returning from Kompong Som. The SOC claimed security forces stopped Ieng Mouli as part of a local police dragnet for armed robbers; UNTAC sources described it as a premeditated attack.

A member of an independent Cambodian human rights organization L'association des droits de l'homme au Cambodge, or AD-HOC, was arrested and interrogated on May 1, and police confiscated the application papers and photographs of more than thirty persons who wanted to become members. UNTAC investigated the incident and received assurances that no further arrests would take place, but other members of the group received threats that if they continued to report to UNTAC, they might "meet with an accident."

The still-limited tolerance for freedom of expression and association, let alone dissent, makes it imperative that no party have the ability to track the political activities of Cambodians. Apparently since the inception of the PRK, the Phnom Penh government has issued identity cards for citizens that by a code number are linked to extensive political dossiers. These dossiers, kept in a government office in the district of residence, have the potential for abuse, especially during a political campaign, by giving the SOC the means to identify people by political profile for the purposes of recruitment, coercion, or intimidation. The return of Cambodians from the border camps has raised a new problem: unless they can get an SOC identity card, they will be instantly recognizable as refugees (and therefore affiliated to a potentially hostile resistance faction) through either a temporary UN card or the ration books they used in the camps. The solution is to keep the identity card system but to destroy existing political dossiers.

Racial Violence. Three centuries of political subjugation and loss of territory to Vietnam lie behind the almost pathological fear and hatred that Cambodians bear their dominant neighbor. This historic enmity has been raised to a new pitch by continuous propaganda by the resistance factions that Vietnamese soldiers, disguised as civilians or as soldiers of the Phnom Penh army, are present and preparing to annex the country. At least two massacres of Vietnamese civilians have occurred since UNTAC's arrival, and the Khmer Rouge ominously warn of more should its demands for the expulsion of Vietnamese civilians not be met.

The Khmer Rouge claims that two million Vietnamese are now living inside Cambodia; Prince Ranariddh, of the FUNCINPEC, claims over one million are present, including forty thousand troops and "illegal people";[14] the KPNLF echoes the one million figure.[15] In contrast, Vietnam claims about one hundred thousand Vietnamese settlers in the country,[16] and most independent observers put the estimate between two hundred and five hundred thousand.[17] Vietnamese have lived in Cambodia for generations, intermarrying with Cambodians and working as small traders or fishermen. The KPNLF, whose leadership is drawn largely from Lon Nol-era officials, is fond of claiming that all Vietnamese in the country are present illegally, citing an agreement between the Lon Nol regime and the government of South Vietnam for the deportation of ethnic Vietnamese from Cambodia. The Khmer Rouge continued the slaughter of ethnic Vietnamese during its reign, in which most of the remaining community fled to Vietnam. Since the defeat of the Khmer Rouge, many of the Khmer-speaking Vietnamese community have returned to their homes, and there is no doubt that UNTAC's arrival and the current economic boom in Phnom Penh have drawn new migrants in search of work in construction and other industries (including prostitution).

The expulsion of all ethnic Vietnamese from Cambodia has been one of the conditions set by the Khmer Rouge for cooperation with the peace plan. To date, the party has presented no credible evidence of a Vietnamese military presence in the country, although UNTAC has made a major effort to facilitate the identification of Vietnamese forces by creating mobile units to investigate possible claims. The theme of a massive Vietnamese troop presence in the country has been a staple of Khmer Rouge propaganda well after Vietnam's 1989 withdrawal of most of its forces. Recently, its focus has shifted to the alleged threat of Vietnamese troops disguising themselves as civilians, and it continues to play masterfully on Cambodian fears of racial extinction through the prospect that Vietnam will annex the rest of the country just as it did Kampuchea Kraom, a large part of southern Vietnam that was Cambodian territory only a century ago.[18]

Khmer Rouge leaders have claimed the Phnom Penh government is "naturalizing" one million Vietnamese so that they may vote in the elections, and that "Vietnamese aggressors" have taken up residence in Phnom Penh "disguised . . . as pedicab operators, bicycle repairers, motorcycle and car mechanics, sellers of radios, televisions, and cars, and so on,"[19] or that in Kompong Cham province "countless Yuon" are "hiding out along river banks and in boats, floating houses, shop houses and townships" as soldiers in civilian guise.[20]

While the Khmer Rouge churns out the most vituperative and unrelenting invective against ethnic Vietnamese, leaders of the KPNLF and FUNCINPEC have been quick to join in, sensing a winning campaign theme. Ieng Mouli, secretary general of the executive committee of the KPNLF and a member of the SNC, has proposed various degrading tests to ferret out Vietnamese disguised as Cambodians, from listening to their accent or asking them to chant a Buddhist prayer to having women run a hundred meters in a sarong, on the theory that it will come undone on a Vietnamese woman.[21] Son Sann, president of the KPNLF, has called on the Yuon to go back to Vietnam, claiming that the Vietnamese should not be allowed to grab all the fertile land, hold all the good jobs, plunder Cambodian resources, and seize "no one knows how many regions in Cambodia."[22] Prince Ranariddh, of the FUNCINPEC, has also charged that the Vietnamese are disguised as Phnom Penh government soldiers, that they are organized in networks in direct contact with Saigon, and that "there are weapons in all Vietnamese houses and boathouses."[23]

The escalating campaign of hatred has already claimed the lives of Vietnamese civilians. In April and May 1992 Khmer Rouge units struck at the predominantly Vietnamese fishing village of Kok Kandal in Kompong Chhnang province, killing seven civilians. Nearly half of the three thousand villagers have fled to the provincial capital and Phnom Penh.[24] On July 21 a premeditated massacre was carried out in the village of Tuk Meas in Kampot province by uniformed men wielding assault rifles and grenades. According to UN sources, the assailants fired into a group of villagers at close range, killing seven, including a woman who fell on top of her seven-day-old baby, crushing the child's skull. Although some news reports blamed renegade soldiers of the Phnom Penh government, the UN investigation showed circumstantial evidence suggesting the assailants were Khmer Rouge.[25] The Khmer Rouge, in turn, denied responsibility, instead crediting "Cambodian soldiers" who "with outrage at the Vietnamese aggressors' systematic plundering of their parents and relatives, have become impatient," and declared "the fury of the local people and Cambodian soldiers is extremely fierce at present."[26]

The call for the expulsion of ethnic Vietnamese has such clear potential to undermine UNTAC's authority and the fragile cooperation of the other Cambodian parties that it is not surprising that both Hun Sen and Yasushi Akashi have scheduled talks with the government of Vietnam.[27] One fear is that by unleashing a pogrom against the Vietnamese, the Khmer Rouge hopes to draw Vietnam back into Cambodia in some fashion and use its presence to garner further support as the most ultranationalist of the factions. So potent is the anti-Vietnamese incitement that the Phnom Penh government has kept an extremely low profile. According to the *Far Eastern Economic Review,* Prime Minister Hun Sen, in passing along reports of demonstrations the resistance parties were planning against Vietnamese residents of Phnom Penh, warned that UNTAC would have to rely on its own police, as SOC police would not intervene.[28]

In dealing with this problem, UNTAC is in a quandary. Hatred of the Vietnamese runs so deep within Cambodian society that racist invective is received in almost every circle with approval; even civil servants of the current Phnom Penh government who suffered terribly at the hands of the Khmer Rouge admire the party's uncompromising attacks. According to one journalist, Phnom Penh residents have begun to call UNTAC "YuonTAC," in reference to its close workings with the SOC government and the common sight of UNTAC soldiers with Vietnamese prostitutes.[29] Control of racist speech that is an incitement to violence is part of UNTAC's mandate, yet such control will be extremely difficult to exercise without creating either a censorship agency or sympathy for those who are sanctioned.

Further violence against the Vietnamese is inevitable unless UNTAC gives priority for police protection to Vietnamese communities and vigorously pursues investigations into anti-Vietnamese violence.

Complaint Procedures and Investigations of Human Rights Abuses. The Paris Agreements empower UNTAC to provide for the "investigation of human rights complaints, and, where appropriate, corrective action."[30] The UNTAC note approved by the SNC in early April authorizes UNTAC investigators to go to the scene where serious violations are alleged and interview victims, witnesses, and any investigating officers. Between April and August 1992 the UNTAC human rights component received almost two hundred complaints at its Phnom Penh and provincial offices. Almost half of these complaints concerned land disputes, which for the most part had been referred to the civilian administration component or the police. The human rights office has investigated allegations of killings, political harassment, wrongful imprisonment, and assault, and when necessary, has recommended corrective action. SOC authorities have generally been cooperative, and more than one hundred wrongfully held detainees have been released as a result. Although it has not reported on the results of specific investigations, the human rights office does include information on how to make complaints in educational materials it disseminates through leaflets, radio broadcasts, and videotapes.

The Future

UNTAC has a heavy and perhaps unrealistic burden in tackling long-entrenched human rights abuses, which must be addressed before a politically neutral atmosphere can be created. It must also tackle the problems that the peace process itself has thrown up, from greater political space for the Khmer Rouge to increased racial hatred of the Vietnamese. UNTAC is not a miracle worker, and it needs the sustained moral and material support of the international community to encourage the emergence of other institutions that can help in the task of human rights protection.

The most important task as well as the most difficult for the immediate future is to put together and enforce a set of sanctions that will either bring the Khmer Rouge into the peace process or effectively address the political and security threat the Khmer Rouge represents. As long as Khmer Rouge forces continue to gain political ground, protection of human rights is problematic.

Getting a functioning legal system in order should be a top priority. The Asia Foundation is already involved in assisting legal education, primarily by sending in Americans to teach. The new penal code being drawn up by UNTAC is loosely based on a French or civil law model. Given the many strands of law and legal practice that Cambodians have been exposed to, from the French to the Soviet to the Anglo-American, some overall coordination is needed, which UNTAC may be able to provide. But the international community must recognize that the task of preparing Cambodia to be a country where the rule of law holds sway cannot be accomplished within the time frame proposed under the Paris Agreements; long-term support of the reconstruction of the legal system is therefore crucial.

Since the protection of human rights depends to some extent on the concepts of due process and equal protection under the law and the notion that individuals whose rights have been violated have some channel of obtaining redress, it is important that an alternative arbiter be available until a functioning and impartial legal system is in place. This resolution may involve a long-term UN presence beyond the life of UNTAC. Another possibility would be for the SNC to accede to the Optional Protocol on the International Covenant on Civil and Political Rights, which enables individuals to raise complaints with a human rights committee set up under the covenant, if all domestic remedies have failed. A third option, but one that might well be politically untenable, would be to involve expatriate judges under UN supervision in an appeals process, or to allow visiting judges to serve on Cambodian courts until a critical mass of trained Cambodians is in place.

The growth of nongovernmental organizations and associations needs to be encouraged as a "voice of the voiceless" and channel for conveying concerns and information between grassroots and center, and as a check on the government. If the UN agencies or the new government for tactical reasons shies away from publicizing human rights abuses and bringing about change, pressure from below may be effective. (It may be self-evident, but the idea of freedom of association can best be encouraged by a proliferation of associations, free of political control.)

Many Cambodia experts have seen the reemergence of the Buddhist *sangha* as highly significant in this regard, with the monkhood having the potential to play a role in human rights monitoring akin to that played by the Catholic church in Latin America or the Philippines. This circumstance is unlikely to happen in the near term, partly because the SOC is determined that the sangha restrict itself to purely traditional activities. But whether or not it becomes involved in human rights work, the sangha may eventually become one of the strongest independent nongovernmental associations in the country; at the very least, it may help provide the cultural filter through which notions of rights and obligations are conveyed.

As of this writing, three human rights organizations had emerged (one of which, ADHOC, is based in a Buddhist temple) and two were in the process of formation. They need as much contact as possible with their counterparts in the region, especially in Thailand, and training in public education or documentation and analysis, depending on their chosen role.

Access to independent sources of Khmer-language reporting on and analysis of domestic and external developments relating to Cambodia is crucial. It is also essential that returning refugees have access to full information about the options they have in terms of resettlement, so they are not persuaded by deliberate disinformation to choose a destination where their rights are less likely to be protected. To this end, the international community should give full support to the establishment of a UN radio station ("Voice of UNTAC") for which Akashi has already requested additional international funding. Donor agencies could also subsidize the publication of Khmer-language bulletins or newspapers not associated with a particular political faction and expose editors through training sessions to the power of investigative journalism while UNTAC is still in place to protect them.

It is accepted wisdom in the international human rights community that investigation, prosecution, and punishment of particularly grave human rights offenses—political killings, disappearances, and torture—are essential to deter such abuses in the future. Even before the judicial system is fully operative, there may have to be a kind of triage system for selection of cases to try, and gross human rights abuses should be given priority, with perhaps one court in Phnom Penh reserved for trying these cases. Another possibility would be to fund a system of mobile courts to go into areas where, at present, a permanent court would be impractical. Commitments on paper to uphold international human rights agreements will be meaningless unless they can be enforced. One can imagine the execution in a Khmer Rouge-held area of a villager accused of being a Vietnamese spy or the killing in a KPNLF area of someone suspected of aiding the Khmer Rouge. How will UNTAC or its successors gain access to these areas to investigate, and who would dare to talk in the face of likely reprisals against self and family members? Yet if the murder goes unpunished, it may lead to more killings, greater fear, and a general escalation in political violence.

If prosecution of all cases is impractical, disclosure of abuses becomes even more important. UNTAC's human rights component or, after UNTAC's departure, the special rapporteur on Cambodia, to be appointed by the UN Commission on Human Rights in Geneva, will have primary responsibility for investigations, and it is critically important that reports of those investigations be published, not suppressed in the interest of keeping the peace.

At some stage a new government in Cambodia will have to come to terms with the Khmer Rouge past. Pol Pot and his inner circle—Ieng Sary, Ta Mok, Son Sen, and Khieu Samphan—deserve to be tried for crimes against humanity. To guarantee impartiality, however, the trials would have to be held outside Cambodia, but international support for such a move is unlikely as long as any hope remains that the Paris Agreements can be implemented. Even then, there will be a question of where responsibility for the atrocities of 1975-79 begins and ends. The last thing Cambodia needs is another witch hunt.

A word needs to be said about corruption. A deeply corrupt

society is not conducive to respect for human rights, and Cambodia is no exception. The arrival of thousands of UNTAC personnel is pumping hitherto unimaginable sums of money into the economy and the black market, giving a major campaign platform to the Khmer Rouge in the process. Land values have skyrocketed, fueling land disputes that have become the major category of complaints submitted to UNTAC's human rights component. Anything and everything is up for sale, including Cambodian identification cards that Thai businesspeople can use to buy property. In 1990-91 widespread corruption eroded the legitimacy of the Hun Sen government. Even if UNTAC personnel remain untainted, the corruption feeding off the UN presence may eventually undercut UNTAC's legitimacy as well. It can undermine the integrity of institutions that might otherwise protect human rights, such as the police and courts, if justice can be bought. It raises the possibility that high-ranking government officials will be able to turn political power into economic power, as former Communist Party officials have done in Eastern Europe, or that Thai payoffs to military commanders of the former resistance factions will prop up repressive fiefdoms in the northwest, or that if an election does take place in 1993, votes will go to the highest bidder.

Protection of human rights in Cambodia is not a question of reconstruction, rebuilding something damaged or destroyed; it is a question of construction, putting in place what was not there before. The ability to criticize authority, to challenge misguided policies or offer alternative ideas, to speak out without fear of reprisal, arrest, or execution, and to demand redress for wrongs suffered at the hands of the state was not much in evidence in Cambodia even before the Khmer Rouge came to power. It will not magically come into being with a free election. Nor will it emerge automatically from a process of economic development. It needs to be nurtured, but it may prove to be as critical to the future of Cambodia as a rebuilt infrastructure or a highly skilled workforce.

Notes

1. David P. Chandler, *The Tragedy of Cambodian History: Politics, War and Revolution Since 1945* (New Haven, Conn.: Yale University Press, 1991): 93.
2. Ibid., 183.
3. Ibid., 203.
4. Elizabeth Becker, *When the War Was Over* (New York: Simon and Schuster, 1986): 21.
5. The two approaches, both of which are valid, are represented by Eva Mysliwiec, *Punishing the Poor* (Oxford: Oxfam, 1988), and Amnesty International, *Kampuchea: Political Imprisonment and Torture* (London: Amnesty International, 1987). See also Sidney Jones, "War and Human Rights in Cambodia," *New York Review of Books*, 19 July 1990, 12.
6. *Indochina Digest*, 1 November 1991.
7. Bob Maat, *The Weight of These Sad Times: "End of Mission" Report on the Thai-Kampuchean Border, December 8, 1979-April 30, 1989*, appendix (privately published manuscript).
8. Asia Watch, *Violations of the Laws of War by the Khmer Rouge,* February 1990; Asia Watch, *Khmer Rouge Abuses Along the Thai-Cambodian Border* (New York: Human Rights Watch, 1989). See also Lawyers' Committee for Human Rights, *Seeking Shelter: Cambodians in Thailand* (New York: Lawyers' Committee for Human Rights, 1987); Lawyers' Committee for Human Rights, *Refuge Denied: Problems in the Protection of Vietnamese and Cambodians in Thailand and the Admission of Indochinese Refugees into the United States* (New York: Lawyers' Committee for Human Rights, 1989).
9. Sonny Imbaraj, "Khmer Rouge Increases Forces Near Site 8," *The Nation* (Bangkok), 24 October 1991; Kokhet Chanthaoletlak, "Refugees to Move to Khmer Rouge Areas," *The Nation*, 28 October 1991.
10. Lawyers' Committee for Human Rights, *Cambodia: The Justice System and Violations of Human Rights* (New York: Lawyers' Committee for Human Rights, 1992): 44-45.
11. United Nations High Commissioner for Refugees, Minutes

of In-house Meeting on Revision of Planning Assumptions and Strategy for Cambodian Repatriation, 3 and 6 January 1992.

12. Christophe Peschoux, *Enquete sur les "nouveaux" Khmers Rouges*, 86-87.

13. Asia Watch, *Political Control, Human Rights, and the UN Mission in Cambodia,* September 1992, 43.

14. He based this estimate on the assumption that three hundred Vietnamese entered the country each day over the last thirteen years. "Ranariddh Interviewed on Non-Aligned Movement, Peace Process," *(Clandestine) Voice of the Khmer in Cambodian*, 22 May 1992 (Foreign Broadcast Information Service transcript FBIS-EAS-92-101, 26 May 1992).

15. "Son Sann Reports on Australia, ASEAN Tour," *(Clandestine) Voice of the Khmer in Cambodian*, 21 May 1992 (Foreign Broadcast Information Service transcript FBIS-EAS-92-102, 27 May 1992).

16. "Voting Rights for Vietnamese Settlers Demanded," *Phnom Penh Samleng Pracheachon Kampuchea in English*, 19 May 1992 (Foreign Broadcast Information Service transcript FBIS-EAS-92-097, 19 May 1992).

17. See Nayan Chanda, "Wounds of History," *Far Eastern Economic Review*, 30 July 1992, 15-16.

18. In a letter to Prince Sihanouk, Khieu Samphan warned that if the Vietnamese were allowed to remain in Cambodia, "more of them will be sent to Cambodia one or two million at a time until their numbers make up one-eighth, two-eighths, three-eighths, four-eighths, and five-eighths of the Cambodian population. In such a case, Cambodia and the Cambodian people will be Vietnamized through Vietnam's strategy of annexing Cambodia and the Cambodian people." "Khieu Samphan Explains Stances to Sihanouk," *(Clandestine) Voice of the Great National Union Front of Cambodia (in Cambodian),* 5 June 1992 (Foreign Broadcast Information Service transcript FBIS-EAS-92-110, 8 June 1992).

19. "Regime Naturalizing Vietnamese Before Elections," *(Clandestine) Voice of the Great National Union Front of Cambodia (in Cambodian),* 20 May 1992 (Foreign Broadcast Information Service

transcript FBIS-EAS-92-099, 21 May 1992); "Vietnamese 'Aggressors' Said Living in Phnom Penh," *(Clandestine) Voice of the Great National Union Front of Cambodia (in Cambodian)*, 20 May 1992 (Foreign Broadcast Information Service transcript FBIS-EAS-92-099, 21 May 1992).

20. "Clandestine Vietnamese Presence Condemned," *(Clandestine) Voice of the Great National Union Front of Cambodia (in Cambodian)*, 18 June 1992 (Foreign Broadcast Information Service transcript FBIS-EAS-92-119, 19 June 1992).

21. Chanda, "Wounds of History," 14.

22. See "28 May Interview with Son Sann Reported," *(Clandestine) Voice of the Khmer in Cambodian*, 3 June 1992 (Foreign Broadcast Information Service transcript FBIS-EAS-92-108, 4 June 1992).

23. "Ranariddh Discusses Tokyo Conference Outcome," *Voice of the Khmer (in Cambodian)*, June 1992 (Foreign Broadcast Information Service transcript FBIS-EAS-92-127, 1 July 1992).

24. "Dark Days at Kok Kandal," *Far Eastern Economic Review*, 30 July 1992, 14.

25. Sue Downie, "Khmer Rouge Suspected in Massacre of Vietnamese," *United Press International*, 20 August 1992.

26. "Khmer Rouge Deny Massacre of Vietnamese," *(Clandestine) Voice of the Great National Union Front of Cambodia*, 29 July 1992 (Foreign Broadcast Information Service transcript FBIS-EAS-92-147, 30 July 1992).

27. Som Sattana, "Phnom Penh Says Khmer Rouge Seeking to Weaken UN in Cambodia," *United Press International*, 11 August 1992; "Cambodian Premier on Private Visit to Vietnam," *Reuters*, 12 August 1992.

28. Chanda, "Wounds of History," 16.

29. Jacques Bekaert, "Asia Pacific Focus," *Bangkok Post*, 22 August 1992, reprinted in Foreign Broadcast Information Service transcript FBIS-EAS-92-165, 25 August 1992.

30. Agreements on a Comprehensive Political Settlement on the Cambodia Conflict, annex 1, section E(c), UN Document DPI/1180, 23 October 1991.

IV

The Cambodian Legal System: An Overview

Dolores A. Donovan

If not for the Khmer Rouge, institutions of law in Cambodia would still be standing. Legislators, prosecutors, judges, lawyers, and law professors were killed or forced to flee the country. Law books were destroyed and the buildings that had housed the courts and the law school converted to other uses. Estimates of the number of legal professionals remaining in Cambodia at the end of the massacres in 1978 range from six to ten. In short, Cambodia's formal legal system was completely destroyed by the Khmer Rouge.[1]

The Cambodian legal system is based on the ancient Asian model of community-based, nonadversarial dispute resolution through conciliation. The French, whose midnineteenth-century arrival in Cambodia is recent when viewed against the backdrop of a Cambodian civilization flourishing in the ninth century a.d., superimposed a formal legislative and judicial system on the preexisting Khmer conciliation system. It is this French system, which was retained after Cambodia's declaration of independence from France in 1945, that was destroyed by the Khmer Rouge in the period 1975-78. The traditional conciliation system also disintegrated during these years, as did all of Khmer society. Only recently, as Khmer communities have re-formed, has conciliation once again begun to flourish.

In 1980 the People's Republic of Kampuchea (PRK), which had been installed by Vietnam after its invasion of Cambodia and ouster of the Khmer Rouge, began to rebuild a formal court system. Because that government, like many socialist regimes, devalued law, it was slow to rebuild the legal system generally and to restore legal education in particular. The few laws that were enacted and courts that were created bore the imprint of Soviet concepts of socialist legality.[2] In 1989 the PRK changed its name to the State of Cambodia (SOC), with Hun Sen as prime minister. Under the Hun Sen regime the government began to create a functioning legislative and judicial system, but lack of personnel and money prevented any significant progress. The result is that the legal system remains the least developed of Cambodia's political and economic structures.

Today the government of Cambodia[3] is intensifying its efforts to rebuild the country's legal system. Three major issues confront the architects of the legal system as they commence their task of reconstruction. The first and most fundamental is how to remake a legal system in a country without lawyers. The second is how to accomplish, within and by means of legal institutions, the transition from socialism to liberal democracy to which the country has formally committed itself. The third is whether to return Cambodia's legal system to its immediately postcolonial past or forge a new system at once more Khmer and more modern.

A commitment to educate the legal professionals necessary to the operation of a functioning legal system was made by the SOC in the fall of 1991. A commitment to create a liberal democratic legal system was likewise made in the Paris Agreements signed by the four contending Khmer factions on October 23 of that year. The socialist law and legal structures now in place seem likely to be gone within the next few years. The question is with what will they be replaced. The centuries-old conciliation system will continue on as before, needing only structural adjustments in packaging to meet the needs of modern entrepreneurs for commercial mediation and arbitration. The hard choices for the Cambodians lie in the fields of substantive law, procedure, and judicial and prosecutorial process. A return to the French legal system imposed in the colonial era would be the easiest path for the Cambodians to take. The more difficult route would be to explore the other options available, choosing from the legal institutions developed by the democratic nations of the world, then mixing them with traditional Khmer dispute resolution mechanisms to create a legal system that is uniquely Cambodian.

The future of the Cambodian legal system will turn on developments in education, judicial independence, and criminal justice reform. The education required to bring about change is of two sorts: education of a new generation of judges, lawyers, and government officials trained in the concept of a political system governed by the rule of law, and reeducation of the older generation, now in power, in these same concepts. Reeducation of the older generation is of the highest priority, for that generation will draft and implement the constitution and legislation that will shape Cambodia's near future.

The independence of the judiciary and criminal justice reform are very closely linked. The Cambodian judiciary is not now independent; it is subordinated to the executive and legislative branches of government under the socialist theory of unity of powers. Until true separation of powers is achieved, with its necessary corollary of judicial independence, the judiciary, and the courts generally, will be unable to redress and deter abuses of power by the executive branch of government.

Abuses of power by the executive branch of the SOC are most often committed by the police, who, under the direction of the Ministry of the Interior, are charged with the maintenance of law and order. In Cambodia the police operate outside the control of either the judiciary, the procuracy,[4] or the law. Until the police are taught to work within the confines of the law, under the direction of prosecutors and subject to correction by the judiciary, the lawlessness that now characterizes the administration of criminal justice under the SOC (and its successor under a new constitution after the 1993 elections) will continue.

This essay describes the salient features of the Cambodian legal system as it exists today. The essay covers past, present, and future Khmer constitutions, the legislative competency and contributions of the United Nations Transitional Authority in Cambodia (UNTAC), and the present state of legal education, the courts, the legal profession, and the police in Cambodia. The essay also analyzes the function of Cambodian dispute resolution by conciliation, known in the West as alternative dispute resolution, and surveys the major pieces of legislation now in force in Cambodia.

The Constitution

Cambodia declared its independence from France in 1945. Since that time it has had six constitutions: the two Sihanouk constitutions of 1947 and 1956, the Lon Nol constitution of 1972, the Khmer Rouge constitution of 1976, and the two constitutions enacted by the present regime, one in 1981 and one in 1989. The four warring Cambodian factions have agreed, in the Paris Agreements of October 23, 1991, that a seventh constitution will be drafted after the election of a constituent assembly, planned for May 1993.

Cambodia had no need of a constitution prior to 1947, for it had been ruled by a long line of god-kings dating from the Khmer Empire of the ninth through thirteenth century. In the succeeding centuries the power of the Cambodian kings waned and the country fell under the influence of Thailand, Vietnam, and in 1863, the French. The French established a protectorate that endured until World War II.

After the death of King Monivong in 1941, eighteen-year-old Prince Norodom Sihanouk was placed on the throne by the French governor-general of Japanese-occupied Indochina, on the mistaken assumption that Sihanouk would acquiesce in continued colonial rule. In 1945, when the Japanese imprisoned French personnel in Indochina, King Sihanouk seized the opportunity to declare Cambodia an independent state. Soon thereafter, however, the French regained control, leaving Sihanouk on the throne, promising a constituent assembly and permitting the formation of political parties. The constitution of 1947 followed in fairly short order.

In 1954 the Geneva Conference was convened to bring a formal conclusion to the Indochina war, in which Vietnam won its independence from France. One issue at the Geneva Conference was the question of whether Norodom Sihanouk's government, established by and under the protection of France, or the Cambodian resistance government, composed of the victorious Hanoi-dominated Viet Minh and members of the Cambodian Communist Party, was the legitimate government of Cambodia. The conference determined that the Sihanouk government was legitimate. In 1955 King Sihanouk abdicated the throne in favor of his father, Norodom Suramarit, in order to enter politics full time, retaking the title "Prince" Sihanouk.

The Sihanouk constitutions of 1947 and 1956 were cut from the same cloth. The constitution of 1956 was an amended version of the 1947 constitution. The 1956 version was referred to as a separate constitution only for historical reasons: Cambodia had achieved independence from the French Union and the existing constitution of the Kingdom of Cambodia was necessarily amended to reflect that fact.[5]

The 1947 constitution established a constitutional monarchy having a bicameral legislative body, an executive power derived from the legislature, and an independent judiciary.[6] The 1956 amendments strengthened the executive power relative to the legislature. Individual political rights were guaranteed. Buddhism was declared the state religion. One highly unusual feature was the provision that all adult citizens of Cambodia, of either sex, may gather twice yearly in a national congress, convoked by the president of the Council of Ministers, to make the citizens' views on matters of national interest known to the government and to the National Assembly.

The 1956 constitution remained in effect until 1970, when Lieutenant General Lon Nol, supported by the United States, seized power from Sihanouk in a military coup. Lon Nol abolished the monarchy and named himself the premier of the new Khmer Republic. The short-lived 1972 Lon Nol constitution[7] was suspended by a declaration of national emergency only one year after it went into effect. It was the only one of the six Khmer constitutions to establish a presidential regime and to provide for a modern, European-style constitutional court empowered to rule on the constitutionality of laws. The 1972 constitution, like the present SOC constitution, declared Buddhism the state religion.

In April 1975 the Lon Nol government was overthrown by the Khmer Rouge, who established the People's Republic of Democratic Kampuchea. The Khmer Rouge is the faction, led by members of the Cambodian Communist Party, that controlled Cambodia (or Kampuchea, as the faction called it) from April 1975 through December 1978. Espousing the political tenets of radical Marxism-Leninism-Maoism, it sought to remove all vestiges of modern Western civilization from Cambodia in order to create an agrarian communist utopia. In the process of purging Cambodia of all Western influence, the Khmer Rouge killed, or caused the deaths by starvation of, an estimated eight hundred thousand to one million Cambodians. The total Cambodian population prior to the Khmer Rouge regime was approximately seven million.

The 1976 Khmer Rouge constitution[8] was, as one might have expected, a radical Maoist document. State institutions were minimal. Where they existed they were, more often than not, charged with maintaining political correctness rather than performing more traditional state functions. The courts, for example, existed to monitor "activities . . . characterized by their systematic and dangerous attitude toward the people's state."[9]

Between 1977 and 1979 a number of Khmer Rouge commanders, including Heng Samrin, Chea Sim, and Hun Sen, fled to Vietnam to escape the internal purges being conducted by Pol Pot, the paramount Khmer Rouge leader. In 1979 they returned with the Vietnamese army that drove the Khmer Rouge out of Phnom Penh and eventually into Thailand. Heng Samrin became the president of the new Vietnamese-backed People's Republic of Kampuchea. Chea Sim became head of the Khmer People's Revolutionary Party (KPRP). Hun Sen, then in his late twenties, was appointed foreign minister; he became prime minister in 1985. In 1981 the People's Republic of Kampuchea promulgated a constitution, superseded in 1989 by the constitution now in effect.

The 1989 constitution[10] presently in force, like its 1981 predecessor, is a socialist document with some liberal tendencies. The 1989 constitution is socialist in that it creates a modified command economy and conditions the exercise of the critical rights of speech, press, and assembly on the observance of "good mores and the customs of society, public social order and national security." Further, the judiciary is subordinated to the legislative branch, with the power of interpretation of the laws reserved to the Standing Committee of the National Assembly. The 1989 constitution's liberal tendencies, at least on paper, can be seen in its affirmation of the right to freedom of faith, the affirmation of a limited right to private property,[11] and the relatively detailed attention given to judicial process and procedure. One unusual provision that to Western eyes is antidemocratic (but that to the Khmer is anticommunist) is article 6 establishing Buddhism as the state religion.

The 1989 constitution, intended as a transitional document marking the departure of the Vietnamese from Cambodia, was followed in 1991 by a restructuring of the Phnom Penh regime. The Hun Sen regime is controlled by the Cambodian People's Party (CPP), the new name adopted October 18, 1991, by the former KPRP. Chea Sim is still the president of the CPP (and chairman of the National Assembly), and Hun Sen is its vice president. Heng Samrin has become the honorary president of the CPP. The CPP is on public record as supporting "a democratic and free political system, a multi-party system with three centres of power: the legislative, the executive and the [judicial] tribunal and a National Assembly elected by the people through universal suffrage and secret balloting and with a free market economy...."[12] Critics of the CPP question the good faith of these avowals.

Civil war has battered Cambodia for more than twenty years. There are at present four major political factions, each with its own armed forces, vying for control of the country. They are the SOC; the National United Front for an Independent, Neutral, Peaceful and Cooperative Cambodia (FUNCINPEC); the Khmer People's National Liberation Front (KPNLF); and the Khmer Rouge. The latter three factions, forming the resistance to the SOC, published their own views on appropriate constitutional principles for Cambodia in 1989. This four-page document, titled "General Principles for a Draft Constitution for Cambodia after Liberation," adopts the principles of liberal democracy in the most general terms; provides for a mixed parliamentary and presidential system reminiscent of the French Fifth Republic; and espouses, in somewhat contradictory terms, a limited form of a priori judicial review of the constitutionality of the laws by a Supreme Court.

On October 23 all four factions signed a peace agreement, brokered by the five permanent members of the United Nations Security Council. In the Paris Agreements the Phnom Penh government, the Sihanoukists, and the Khmer Rouge, all of whom had, in the past, espoused socialism to one degree or another, joined the KPNLF in committing themselves to the key features of liberal democracy, including a multiparty system, an independent judiciary, and a market economy. The Paris Agreements also provide for free elections in 1993, in which all four factions will field candidates, to elect a National Assembly that will write a new constitution for Cambodia.

In the interim, drafts of this new constitution are being prepared by each of the factions at the request and under the supervision of the United Nations Transitional Authority in Cambodia. The form and substance of the seventh constitution is a matter of much current debate in Phnom Penh and among the United Nations personnel charged with the task of assisting Cambodia in its transition to democracy. The Paris Agreements provide that the new constitution is to be drafted within three months of the 1993 elections. Once the constitution has been approved by the duly elected constituent assembly, that assembly is to transform itself into a legislative assembly from which the new Cambodian government will be formed. The four Cambodian factions have agreed that certain fundamental principles must be included in the new constitution, that the constitution (1) will be the supreme law of the land; (2) will provide special protection for human rights, defined to include most of the individual rights familiar to Westerners, such as speech, association, assembly, religion, property, due process, and equality; (3) will affirm Cambodia's sovereignty, independence, neutrality, and national unity; (4) will provide that Cambodia follow a system of liberal democracy on the basis of pluralism; (5) will establish an independent judiciary, empowered to enforce the individual rights provided under the constitution; and (6) must be adopted by a two-thirds majority of the members of the constituent assembly.[13]

These provisions establish that the forthcoming seventh constitution should have many of the earmarks of a liberal democratic document. It has been proven time and again, however, that constitutional recitations of individual rights and assertions that a judiciary is independent do not ensure that fundamental human rights will be protected or that a society will function as a true democracy. The constitution and human rights abuses of the former Soviet Union, or those of Argentina in the late 1970s, illustrate this point. Many critical matters remain to be resolved by the four factions in the course of the drafting process. Although all of the factions now claim to have embraced democratic pluralism and a market economy, their past constitutional practices can nonetheless provide some guidance as to what constitutional models they may be expected to espouse in the drafting process.

Potential differences of opinion emerge from this survey of past Khmer constitutions in two areas: individual rights and the structural relation of the three branches of government. As to individual rights, the issues include (1) whether the state will be empowered to limit the exercise of individual rights in the name of the public welfare and, if so, to what extent; (2) whether economic and social welfare rights, such as the rights to housing, education, and medical care, will be guaranteed, or whether only political rights will be given constitutional status; (3) whether private property rights will be guaranteed and, if so, to what extent; (4) whether freedom of the press will be guaranteed; and (5) whether the state will be empowered to prohibit the exercise of individual rights pursuant to a declaration of state of siege or national emergency.

The second area of potential discord, the structural relationship between the three branches of government, involves these issues: (1) whether the executive power should be elected by universal suffrage separately from the legislative power, as in an American-style presidential regime, or whether the executive power should be derived from the legislative power, as in the traditional European parliamentary model, or whether the two systems should be combined, as in the French Fifth Republic; (2) whether the executive branch, as well as the legislative branch, should have law-making power; (3) whether the judiciary will be elected or appointed and, if the latter, by whom and for what term of office; and (4) whether the judiciary will be empowered to review legislative enactments, executive decrees and regulations, and the actions of officers of the executive branch for conformity with the constitution and, if so, by means of what model of judicial review. One final and overriding question is whether the government may suspend all or some of the constitution by a declaration of state of siege or national emergency and, if so, when may such a declaration be properly issued.

These issues are only the first of the myriad questions of governance that the Khmer must resolve in the next two years. The twenty long years of civil war and the massacres by the Khmer Rouge have left the Khmer with very few persons having the educational background necessary to the task at hand. In the realm of constitution drafting, as in all areas of Cambodian life, the shortage of educated persons may prevent Cambodia from achieving its goal: a seventh constitution that is a viable document under which the Khmer can live in peace.

The Supreme National Council and the United Nations Transitional Authority in Cambodia

On October 23, 1991, the international community, at the Paris International Conference on Cambodia (PICC), placed two nonindigenous governmental institutions at the head of Cambodia's political and legal system. The first of these is the Supreme National Council (SNC), in which reposes, until elections in 1993, Cambodia's sovereignty. The second is the United Nations Transitional Authority in Cambodia, which has the task of monitoring and assisting Cambodia's transition to democracy.

These institutions have, at least until mid-1993, a form of hybrid legislative and executive competency that is very broad. The SNC has delegated to UNTAC all powers necessary to ensure the implementation of the Paris Agreements.[14] Thus, UNTAC has the power, in consultation with the SNC, to supervise the police "and other law enforcement and judicial processes throughout Cambodia" to the extent necessary to ensure that law and order are maintained and that human rights and freedoms are fully protected.[15] UNTAC has boldly interpreted these provisions as justifying the exercise of possibly the most sweeping control over the internal affairs of a nation ever asserted by an international body. The French and American lawyers of UNTAC have drafted both a media charter and a far-reaching, though brief, set of criminal justice provisions having the potential to reconstruct the Cambodian judicial system in general, and the criminal justice system in particular, into a legal system very much in the liberal democratic mode. On September 9, 1992, the SNC, overriding a Khmer Rouge dissent, adopted UNTAC's rules of criminal justice. Should these rules endure past the 1993 elections, they will have a major impact on Cambodia's political and legal landscape.

In the realm of elections, the provisions conferring legislative and executive authority on UNTAC and, to a lesser extent, the SNC are two in number. First, UNTAC, in consultation with the SNC, has the authority to establish "a system of laws, procedures and administrative measures necessary for the holding of a free and fair election in Cambodia, including the adoption of an electoral law and of a code of conduct regulating participation in the election in a manner consistent with respect for human rights and prohibiting coercion or financial inducement in order to influence voter preference."[16] In the elections area, as in the areas of criminal justice and the press, UNTAC has prepared rules of procedure. Second, also in consultation with the SNC, UNTAC has the sweeping power to suspend or abrogate the provisions of existing laws "which could defeat the objects and purposes of this Agreement."[17]

The creation of a new quasi-legislative competency in Cambodia was only one part of the comprehensive settlement negotiated at the PICC. The settlement includes an enhanced UN role in the interim administrative and military arrangements to be put in place before elections are held under UN auspices. The UN role is intended to do only that which is necessary to establish a legitimate government. The Agreements also stress the importance of human rights protection and international guarantees for the terms of a settlement. The settlement includes the following elements: (1) recognition of Cambodia's Supreme National Council, chaired by Prince Sihanouk and comprising individuals who reflect the range of political opinion in Cambodia (i.e., the Sihanoukists, the Khmer People's National Liberation Front, the Phnom Penh regime, and the Khmer Rouge), as the legitimate occupant of Cambodia's seat at the UN until a new government is formed; (2) implementation of a UN-supervised cease-fire, cantonment of the factional military forces, and a phased process of arms control and reduction; and (3) the creation of UNTAC, which would supervise the demilitarization described in (2) above and which would be responsible for the repatriation and resettlement of approximately three hundred fifty thousand refugees now residing on the Thai-Cambodia border. UNTAC would also be responsible for administrative oversight of the SOC's key ministries of defense, foreign affairs, finance, public security (the Ministry of the Interior), and information until a constituent assembly convenes after free and fair elections.

Essentially, the Paris Agreements are intended to enable the Cambodian people to determine their own political future. The Agreements seek to pave the way for the creation of neutral political conditions in Cambodia, allowing all political parties to compete on an equal basis in free and fair elections to be organized and conducted by the UN with full respect for the national sovereignty of Cambodia. Whether or not this scenario will take place, given the political and military realities of Cambodia, is of course an entirely different matter.

In the legal arena, the political infighting and the refusal to disarm will undoubtedly frustrate the UN's realization of its goals in Cambodia. The rules of criminal law and procedure, for example, drafted by UNTAC and approved by the SNC, over Khmer Rouge dissent, contain many of the most fundamental liberal democratic procedural guarantees of due process and human rights. Their approval by the SNC was a major accomplishment by UNTAC, paving the way for the UN to claim at least partial success in fulfilling its mandate of restoring respect for human rights to Cambodia. The approval of these rules, however, must be understood against a backdrop of widespread and continuing human rights abuses by the police forces of the SOC. Such abuses occur wholly outside the legal and judicial system, without the concurrence and often without the knowledge of judges, prosecutors, or the reformers within the SOC government charged with restoration of the rule of law. These human rights abuses will continue, vitiating UNTAC's accomplishments in the criminal justice arena, unless UNTAC directs its attention away from the writing of rules and toward their enforcement.

Legal Education

Since there is almost no written law in Cambodia, the faculty of the national law school, by its choice of what to teach as law, is in a position to redefine the substance of law in Cambodia just as surely as are the drafters of legislation. The process of redefinition will, of course, be more subtle in the educational system, and will be to a large extent subordinate to the more dramatic changes originating in the legislative branch of government. Nonetheless, a major source of the legal, including constitutional, theory that will guide Cambodia's transition from socialism to liberal democracy will be those members of the legal establishment charged with legal education.[18]

During the Sihanouk and Lon Nol eras, legal education was the province of the faculty of law at the University of Phnom Penh. The French system of legal education prevailed, pursuant to which law was taught as an undergraduate discipline, and a law degree, the *license en droit,* conferred upon completion of four years of study. The faculty of law was closely tied to the faculty of economics. Students in law often did a subspecialty in economics and vice versa. In 1975 the Khmer Rouge gutted the campus, leaving only the empty shells of buildings. The books in the law library were destroyed, the desks thrown from the windows, paintings torn from walls. Between 1975 and 1982 there was no legal education inside Cambodia.

In 1982 the government created the Institute of Public Administration and Law (IPAL), located on the former campus of the faculty of law. The mandate from the government was to deliver political and legal education as rapidly as possible to the persons selected to work in the legal system as judges, prosecutors, and justice representatives for conciliation.

The IPAL began by offering a three-month course, which soon became a five-month course, consisting of both Marxist-Leninist philosophy and law, to persons working in the legal system. Approximately 2,350 persons went through the course between 1982 and 1989, when the course was discontinued. In theory, all judges, prosecutors, and justice representatives in Cambodia have taken the course. The purpose of the course appears to have been as much to politically indoctrinate the few remaining university-educated persons to whom the government was forced to turn to staff its courts as to teach them rules of law.

In 1986 a two-year course, culminating in the conferral of a "diploma in law," was added. This diploma in law was not intended to be the equivalent of the bachelor's degree in law, or *license en droit,* formerly awarded by the University of Phnom Penh. This course continued to combine Marxist ideology and economics with law, as had the five-month course, but with a much greater stress on law.[19] For the next three years the five-month course and the two-year course were offered concurrently. In 1989 the five-month course was dropped and only the two-year program remained. A very rough estimate of the number of persons graduating from the two-year course between 1986 and 1991 is between 625 and 750, at a rate of 125 to 150 per year. The content of the curriculum is heavily influenced by the French civil law legal tradition still very much present in Cambodia and Vietnam.[20]

A total of 365 students, 215 in the first year and 150 in the second year, are presently enrolled in the school in the academic year 1991-92. The school has a full-time faculty of five teachers and one academic administrator who is the director. Of the five teachers, three are Khmer who have received their bachelor's degree in law from a Vietnamese university and two are top graduates of the two-year course. The director is one of the three judges under the Sihanouk and Lon Nol regimes who survived the killings of the Khmer Rouge. He holds a bachelor's degree in law from the University of Phnom Penh, with additional legal training in France.

Almost all teaching at the IPAL is done on the European large lecture hall model, which envisions a highly trained academic with a doctoral degree lecturing to one hundred to two hundred students who have prepared for each lecture by reading extensively from assigned texts. The lecture is intended to expand upon and develop theoretical constructs conveyed in basic form by the texts. This lecture hall model is, with only minor variations in format, such as the Socratic technique of questioning employed in the United States, traditional in both the United States and Europe for the basic courses taught in the first and second years of law school. Upper-level courses, which typically begin in the second and third years of graduate-level law school in the United States and in the third and fourth years of undergraduate-level law school in Europe, are ideally taught in a seminar setting, or to classes in the range of thirty-to-forty students.

The IPAL system of instruction departs from the traditional European and American large lecture hall model in that there are few or no texts and no upper-level courses. Moreover, no faculty members hold advanced degrees and some do not hold even university-level degrees. A further problem is the absence of a Khmer-language legal vocabulary adequate to convey complicated legal concepts. Owing to the slaughters by the Khmer Rouge, only four or five persons, the youngest of whom are in their fifties, who speak and write "high Khmer" as it relates to law now remain inside Cambodia. Because of the pressing need for their services in the Ministry of Justice, the courts, and the National Assembly, none of these persons is now teaching at the law school. The combination of all these factors results in an extremely low level of instruction, falling far short of both international standards and the more relaxed standards of developing countries.

The government does not contemplate providing any additional financial, human, or instructional resources to the IPAL. Nonetheless, the government has ordered the IPAL to offer a four-year course of study, presumably adapted to conform to Cambodia's new multiparty political system and its new market economy. This four-year curriculum will culminate in the conferring of the *license en droit,* which is the rough equivalent of a U.S. bachelor of arts degree. The teaching of the new curriculum will begin in October 1992. Three French law professors are expected to arrive in the fall, at the expense of the French government, to assist in the instruction.

One thousand students are now enrolled in a one-year prelaw preparatory class. Of those one thousand, two hundred will be selected, on the basis of performance on a competitive examination, to enter the four-year law course. It is not clear whether graduates of the two-year course will be allowed to participate in the new four-year curriculum.

According to officials in the Ministry of Education in charge of higher education, the law school and the Institute of Economics are to be returned to the University of Phnom Penh in the near future.[21] It is anticipated that restoration of legal education to the university's arts and sciences curriculum will remove the stigma attached to law by the socialist regimes of Cambodia's recent past and promote an understanding of the centrality of the concept of rule of law appropriate to a liberal democratic society.

The Courts, the Legal Profession, and the Police

In the SOC the relationship between the judicial and the executive branches of government is a close one. Pursuant to the theory of unity of powers that is central to socialist political and legal theory, a division of the executive branch, the Ministry of Justice, is charged with supervising the administration of justice in Cambodia. Until 1988 the ministry's supervisorial function included reviewing all judgments rendered by the courts of first instance for factual and legal correctness, and for equity in sentencing. This confusion of the executive and judicial functions and powers has been severely criticized by human rights groups.[22]

In 1988 the function of review of judicial judgments was taken away from the Ministry of Justice and placed in the hands of the newly created Supreme Court. This technical transfer of appellate jurisdiction to the Supreme Court notwithstanding, the judiciary, with the possible exception of certain members of the Supreme Court whose political standing is unusually high, remains subordinate to the officials of the Ministry of Justice in the hierarchy of justice. Neither the courts of first instance nor the Supreme Court has the power to interpret laws and executive decrees or the power to review them for constitutionality. If Cambodia is to achieve its desired transition to a liberal, democratic political and legal system, a high priority in the next few years must be development of an understanding of both the practical implications of the theory of separation of powers and the need for an independent judiciary.

The Courts. The SOC court system is unusual in that there are only two tiers of courts: the courts of first instance and the Supreme Court.[23] There is no right of appeal to the Supreme Court. Thus, although there are several mechanisms for discretionary review by the Supreme Court, there is technically no right to a hearing on appeal in Cambodia. The omission of a right to appeal may be a result of the virtually complete absence of law-trained personnel capable of staffing an appellate system. In addition, the limited number of appeals serves the governmental desire for speed and efficiency in the resolution of disputes within the formal legal system. Another feature of the Cambodian court system that will strike Anglo-Americans as an oddity is that the judiciary and the procuracy are joined together as one organizational entity. This feature, unique to Cambodia, has its origin in socialist legality, derived in turn from principles of continental procedure.

There is a court of first instance in every province in Cambodia, in the city of Kompong Cham, and in the city of Phnom Penh. Only the court of Phnom Penh, which claims to have handled a total of 580 cases in 1990, on a population base of eight hundred thousand, is processing a caseload in any way comparable to a court in an equivalent Asian jurisdiction. Comparisons to Western jurisdictions are inadvisable owing to fundamental differences in societal attitudes toward dispute resolution and toward law. Even after discounting for Asian and Western urban and rural variations, the thirty-six cases handled in 1990 by the provincial court of Kompong Speu, a province with a population of 407,747, is a number so low as to lead to the conclusion that the Kompong Speu court exists only on paper.

The courts of first instance are courts of general jurisdiction, handling both civil and criminal cases. Because the police detain, incarcerate, and in most cases, eventually release persons suspected of crime without ever notifying the procuracy of what they have done, the criminal cases constitute the smallest percentage of the caseload of the courts. Until recently, divorce matters composed by far the largest percentage of cases coming before the Phnom Penh court. In the last year or two, however, the number of contract cases having to do with the purchase, sale, or leasing of real property has risen rapidly.

Attached to each court of first instance is a group of "people's assessors" and a group of "social defenders." These persons hold nonlegal, full-time jobs. When a case comes to trial, two people's assessors are selected to sit on the case with one judge. The three decide the case by majority vote. If the possible sentence in a case is more than five years, one of the social defenders will be appointed to represent the accused person. In theory, the social defenders are also available to assist parties in civil suits. Some of these social defenders are said to be graduates of the five-month course at the Institute of Public Administration and Law.

Each court of first instance sits at the apex of a pyramid of conciliation offices, staffed by persons called justice representatives who conciliate disputes. Although there is a right of appeal from the conciliation offices to the courts of first instance, the vast majority of Cambodian disputes are resolved within the conciliation framework without recourse to the courts.

One military court, located in Phnom Penh, handles all military cases arising throughout Cambodia. The Supreme Court has the power of discretionary review of cases adjudicated by the military court. Very little information can be obtained concerning the functioning of the military court.

The Supreme Court has three chambers: civil, penal, and military. In early 1992 the military chamber had not yet begun to function. The Supreme Court also has two subdepartments: a department of statistics and review and a department of complaints, which the Court operates jointly with the Office of the Procurator-General. This latter department serves, at least in theory, a function similar to that of United States courts charged with reviewing petitions for habeas corpus or complaints for violations of civil rights. Persons who feel that a family member has been wrongfully detained, or that the police have improperly seized their property or invaded their home, are entitled to file a complaint with the procurator-general's office or the

Supreme Court. According to a member of the procurator-general's office, such complaints are on the rise, though still not numerous.

The Legal Profession. If the Western definition of a lawyer were to be applied to Cambodia, only five persons in the entire country would qualify. Since the end of the Khmer Rouge regime in January 1979, the number of fully trained lawyers has actually diminished, owing to the deaths of some of the survivors of the massacres, to five. In the absence of university-level legal education, no members of the younger generation have been trained to replace them.

A preliminary question is thus whether persons who have studied law for only five months, or for only two years, and who work in the courts as judges and prosecutors can be deemed members of the legal profession. In the West the answer given by most lawyers and judges would be no, for the Western concept of a legal professional turns on the prolonged study of a discrete body of knowledge, followed by specialized training and licensing. In developing countries the answer given this question would generally be yes, for in these societies the definition of a legal professional is more functional: if you function as a judge or a prosecutor, you are one. This article adopts the view that a person who is functioning as a judge or prosecutor *is* a member of the legal profession. Such a person may or may not, depending on whether he or she has spent five months or five years in the study of law, be in need of periodic continuing legal education in the areas of substantive law and procedure.

The Cambodian legal profession consists of judges, prosecutors, and law teachers. There are no private lawyers in Cambodia. The intention of the Ministry of Justice officials who created the concept of lay defenders attached to each court is that those defenders would evolve into a corps of private lawyers who would handle both civil and criminal cases. To date, in the SOC there are no signs that the anticipated evolutionary process has begun. On the other hand, the UNTAC rules authorize the creation of a private bar association, and repatriated refugees who have taken law classes in the camps on the Thai-Cambodian border have expressed interest in forming such an association.

Only since 1988, when the Cambodian Supreme Court replaced

the Ministry of Justice as the reviewer of trial court judgments, has the judiciary been allowed any appreciable operational independence. A great deal more remains to be done. It is not clear at this writing whether the majority of judges in Cambodia have any understanding at all of the concept of an independent judiciary. Only with respect to the Supreme Court, the city court of Phnom Penh, and the district court of Kandal Province, immediately adjacent to Phnom Penh, can it be said with certainty that there are sitting judges, educated under the old regime, who are even familiar with the concept of judicial independence.

The total number of judges now on the bench in Cambodia falls into the range of seventy to ninety. The judges are, for the most part, persons with a high school education or a year or two of university-level education, who have passed through the five-month law course offered by the Institute of Public Administration and Law between 1982 and 1989. The number of judges sitting on a court of first instance varies between three and five, depending on the population and caseload of the jurisdiction in question. The most striking aspect of the judicial staffing, both in courts of first instance and in the Supreme Court, has been the number of unfilled judgeships, presumably owing to a lack of qualified candidates.

The judges of the Supreme Court have still not achieved their full complement of nine. Until 1992 only seven judges had been appointed to the Court; in 1992 one more was appointed, for a total of eight. The year 1992 was a milestone in the Court's development, for its president, who until then had been the Court's greatest single liability, was retired and two others, who are among the Court's greatest assets, were appointed, one to become president, the other to fill a vacant vice presidential slot. The Court's enabling legislation provides for a president, three vice presidents, and five judges. Only one vice presidential position remains unfilled.

The new president of the Court was brought out of retirement, at the urging of the liberal reformers in the SOC government, to head the Court. His educational background includes advanced study at the Paris National School of Administration (ENA), as well as a degree in finance from ENA's Cambodian counterpart. The current president is a welcome change from his predecessor, a military man who, prior to his appointment to the Court, held the post of minister of the interior during years in which the forces of the Ministry of the Interior were accused of many serious violations of human rights. The new president's appointment to the Court marks a victory for the forces of law and democracy in Cambodia.

The vice president most recently appointed to the Court, in early 1992, is one of the three judges trained in the law and appointed to the bench in the Sihanouk era who survived the Khmer Rouge period. Expert in law and fluent in French, he is one of the two persons on whom the present regime most relies for advice on legal modernization and reform. He will be the workhorse of the Court, which, without his input, would be unable to handle complex questions of law. The second vice president, also fluent in French, has a degree in finance and public administration from the University of Phnom Penh. He commenced his career in law in 1980 as a judge of the Phnom Penh City Court. His strength is in economic and commercial law. Little is known about the remaining five judges, other than that only one of them is a woman.

The judiciary of Cambodia, with the possible exception of the Supreme Court, operates as a team with the procuracy. The prosecutors, in turn, see themselves as, in fact, an arm of the judiciary. This prosecutorial self-perception is derived in part from the socialist tradition of denominating the prosecutor as a sort of watchdog over the judiciary and in part from the traditional European view of a prosecutor as a "public minister" who, like the judge, must protect the interests of the accused as well as those of law enforcement. French writers have communicated the quasi-judicial status of the prosecutor by informally referring to him or her as *le juge debout* (the judge who stands) and the magistrate as *le juge assis* (the judge who sits).

The number of prosecutors in Cambodia ranges from fifty to sixty. There are typically three prosecutorial positions attached to a court of first instance. Many prosecutorial positions, like judicial positions, are unfilled. The educational level of provincial prosecutors is similar to that of the provincial judiciary.

The central task confronting the prosecutors of Cambodia is to train the police to obey the law. Operation of a criminal justice system in accordance with the law of course turns, ultimately, on the exercise of self-restraint by the police. Self-restraint by the police, however, results in no small part from insistence by prosecutors and judges that the law shall be obeyed, not just by the public, but also by the police. In a socialist system heavily influenced by continental procedure, such as that of Cambodia, the responsibility of supervising the police in their interactions with the courts devolves almost exclusively upon the prosecutorial corps.

The prosecutors of Cambodia have not as yet been able to make visible inroads into the problem of police disregard for the law. They are hampered in their task by the fact that Cambodia is still largely in the lawless condition characteristic of a society emerging from a prolonged civil war, and by the radical socialist tradition of Cambodia's immediate past, which viewed law as subservient to political and military power. Nonetheless, a beginning may have been made.

Procurators at the highest levels are painfully conscious of the lawlessness of the police and of the imperative need to bring the police under control. In the course of a recent discussion of prosecutorial-police relations, a telling comment was made by one of the most senior members of the procurator-general's office. "They are beginning to ask us for authorization to arrest," he said hopefully. "Up until now they have not done so, and that is a violation of the law."[24]

The institutional realities are that the police wield far more power than do the prosecutors. The Cambodian criminal justice system envisions a procedure whereby the police detain a suspect for a short period of time while gathering evidence that satisfies a prosecutor that a formal arrest should be made. Once the arrest has taken place, the case passes from the hands of the police to those of the prosecutor. If the prosecutor is satisfied that the arrested person committed the crime in question, he or she will refer the case to a judge for trial.[25]

This relationship between the police and prosecutors exists in theory only. Informed sources say (and the low number of criminal cases processed by the courts bears them out) that in 90 percent of all criminal cases the police detain a suspect, put the suspect in jail, and keep the suspect there without ever informing the prosecutors of what they have done. Further, another large percentage of minor criminal offenses are processed through the conciliation system, likewise never coming into the hands of the prosecutors.

The Police. The SOC police have been widely characterized as corrupt, brutal, and uncontrollable by any lawful means. The institution that, until 1992, presided over the police was the SOC Ministry of the Interior. That ministry, and hence the police, is supposed to be undergoing a major reorganization under the supervision of UNTAC. Possibly in response to the UNTAC reorganization, the Ministry of the Interior divided itself in mid-1992 into two entities: the Ministry of the Interior and the Ministry of National Security. Only the former is, according to the SOC, within the jurisdiction of UNTAC. The new Ministry of the Interior is charged with matters relating to the administration of provinces and cities, which includes some police work. The new Ministry of National Security, however, is responsible for the bulk of the police work. The division of the police into two parts, one of which may not be subject to UNTAC control, does not bode well for the restoration of law and order to Cambodia.

Although the conduct of the Cambodian police is widely viewed as unprofessional in the extreme, the Ministry of the Interior claims that it operates a police training academy. For the present, whatever training exists has been suspended pending an indication from UNTAC as to what it expects from the ministry in that area. Scant information is available as to the subjects taught at the academy. Courses offered are said to be both short-term, in the range of three to six months, and long-term. The chief of the Ministry of the Interior's Office of Legislation, who doubles as a teacher in the training academy, asserts that law, including human rights law, is taught at the academy.

In the past decade international human rights organizations have accused the Phnom Penh government of numerous violations of human rights. The responsibility for many of these violations can be laid at the door of the police. Fortunately, UNTAC claims that it intends to make the retraining of the police one of its highest priorities; unfortunately, very little evidence of UNTAC action in this regard can yet be seen. It is fair to say that UNTAC's demonstrated inability to control the forces of the Ministry of the Interior has been one of the greatest disappointments of UNTAC's tenure in Cambodia.

The Conciliation Process: Alternative Dispute Resolution

As noted previously, the conciliation process is the heart of the Khmer legal system. Resolution of disputes by conciliation is found everywhere in Cambodian society, both inside and outside the court system. It is fair to say that there are two legal systems in Cambodia, a formal legal system built around the courts and an informal one built around conciliation, with the latter only loosely attached to the state.

The conciliation process operated by the state exists at three levels. Conciliation begins at the village level, where it is conducted by village chiefs, by monks, or by a justice representative who is a state employee, and sometimes by all three at once. Extrajudicial conciliation is reportedly found not only in villages but also in factories and large offices, where it is carried out by a supervisor or other person in authority. Regardless of who carries out the village-level conciliation, there is an informal right of appeal to the next administrative level, the *khum,* or commune. From the commune there is an appeal to the *srok*, or district, and from the district to the provincial court of first instance. The state employees who perform the conciliation function at all levels below the courts of first instance are called justice representatives. Even the judges of the courts of first instance are required to attempt, at least once, to conciliate the cases that come before them, whether the cases are on appeal from the conciliation system or filed directly in the court. The vast majority of cases processed through the state conciliation system were, until very recently, domestic matters involving domestic violence, divorce, and child support.

The Khmer word for the process by which a person in authority resolves a dispute is, phonetically rendered in the Western alphabet, *kar phsas.* The word *conciliation* is the English translation of the French word *reconcilier,* used by French-speaking Khmer in Phnom Penh to describe the form of alternative dispute resolution character-istic of Khmer society. English-speaking Khmer in United Nations

Refugee Camp Site 2 on the Thai-Cambodian border use the English words *conciliation* and *to reconcile* interchangeably to describe the Khmer form of alternative dispute resolution. The question arises whether what the Cambodian justice representatives do is properly called conciliation, which is a form of mediation, or whether the process would more accurately be described as arbitration. The operative principle of mediation is that the mediator assists the parties in working out their own agreement. An arbitrator listens to both sides of the dispute and reaches a decision that may or may not require each side to concede something to the other. Preliminary accounts of the Khmer process in action indicate that what really occurs is not mediation but rather arbitration. In view of the hierarchical nature of Khmer social relations, that reality is not surprising.

The state conciliation network attached to the city court of Phnom Penh is the most highly developed in the country. The urban districts of Phnom Penh are called *khans*, and the neighborhoods into which they are divided *sangkats*. In the fall of 1991 Phnom Penh was divided into four urban khans and three suburban sroks, each with a justice representative and a secretary. The khans were in turn divided into sangkats, each with a justice representative, and the sroks into khums, each with a justice representative, for a total of seventy-seven sangkat-khum justice representatives. Added to the seven khan-srok justice representatives and their secretaries, who also conduct conciliation sessions, the total number of persons in conciliation work in the jurisdiction of Phnom Penh amounts to eighty-eight. The significance of this number is best understood in light of the fact that the Phnom Penh City Court is staffed by only six judges.

The justice representatives, who are authorized to conciliate disputes on behalf of the state, are even less well trained and well educated than the judiciary. It is likely that the majority of justice representatives are not high school graduates, owing not to any lack of native intelligence, but rather to the fact that their education was interrupted by war. Their salaries of approximately eight U.S. dollars per month do not permit them to support their families, and the concept of professional standards of behavior has never been explained to them. It is not surprising, therefore, that allegations of corruption are frequently levied against them.

The state conciliation system, like the court system, is utilized by urban Khmer, but not by persons living in the countryside. This urban-rural division does not mean that the conciliation process does not occur in the countryside, but rather that it occurs outside the state system. In fact, it is fair to say that most Cambodian dispute resolution outside Phnom Penh occurs outside the legal system provided by the state.

This widespread preference for nongovernmental dispute resolution by conciliation arises from many different causes. Some are obvious, such as the inability of government to establish functioning dispute resolution mechanisms in the midst of civil war. Twenty years of civil war have perforce taught the Khmer that they cannot rely on state assistance for the resolution of disputes. Other causes are culturally based, such as the Khmer preference for turning to monks or persons higher up in the social hierarchy for resolution of disputes. Corruption must be included in any list of reasons why the Khmer do not turn to the state for dispute resolution.

In recent years there has been a tremendous upsurge of contract disputes and civil litigation, generated by the general confusion over property rights and the ongoing and still unfinished rewriting of law and regulations relating to real property. The privatization of industry and commerce can be expected to generate even more civil disputes. The sudden presence of twenty thousand UNTAC personnel—all foreigners with cultural and legal heritages far different from the Khmer—will create additional frictions.

The formal legal system is still too undeveloped to bear the increased burden of these civil disputes. The conciliation system is likewise unprepared to handle the new influx of cases. The Cambodian government, forced to choose between developing the courts or developing the conciliation system, is leaning toward the latter alternative.

If the government opts to develop the network of justice representatives into a system capable of handling relatively sophisticated disputes, it will face a gargantuan task. The education and training of the justice representatives will have to be substantially upgraded.

Something less than a four-year university-level legal education for justice representatives should suffice, but certainly a level of familiarity with commercial law and modern dispute resolution not presently found in the ranks of the justice representatives will be required. On the other hand, in a country with no lawyers and a centuries-old tradition of nonadversarial dispute resolution, diversion of a large proportion of civil disputes into a system of alternative dispute resolution makes a great deal of sense. If the government does finally choose to develop the conciliation network into a system capable of handling not only domestic matters and simple contract disputes but also commercial mediation and arbitration, Cambodia will be at the cutting edge of the worldwide movement away from courts into new forms of alternative dispute resolution.

Legislation

Cambodia is at present a society governed almost exclusively by the executive branch of government, through the medium of executive decrees[26] and regulations. The number of actual pieces of legislation, duly enacted by the legislature before promulgation by the executive branch, is very few. Major areas of Cambodian life (ownership of property, for example, which in most countries would be governed by legislative enactments) are controlled by decrees and by regulations issued by the ministries with immediate supervisorial responsibility over the issue in question.[27] This absence of legislation and consequent reliance on ministerial-level officials for decision making that in other societies would fall within the purview of the more publicly visible legislative process is in part responsible for the many allegations of corruption levied against the executive officers of the current government.

The small number of laws on the books makes the enacting of legislation a matter of the highest priority, rivaled only by the need to educate and field enough legal professionals to render Cambodia's legal system operational. It is in the area of legislation that the choices between socialist and democratic legal institutions, and between colonial and modern legal institutions, are most clearly defined. The critical organizational, substantive, and procedural choices now confronting the Cambodian government must be made in the very near future.

Legislation originates in the governmental ministry or institution most concerned with the subject matter of the proposed legislation. The following entities are entitled to initiate legislation: a ministry, the national bank, the Supreme Court, the Office of the Procurator-General, and the members of the National Assembly.[28] If proposed legislation is of interest to two or more institutions or ministries, the entities must collaborate in the drafting.

Once the first draft has been drawn up, the legislation is passed to the Ministry of Justice for review as to form and substance. The draft is then passed to the Council of Ministers,[29] which next submits it to the Council of State. The Council of State submits the legislation to the legislative drafting committee of the National Assembly, which then passes it to the Standing Committee of the National Assembly.[30] Only the National Assembly, by majority vote, has the power to enact legislation.[31] Once legislation is enacted, the Council of State promulgates the law. The Council of Ministers has the duty of disseminating information about the recently promulgated law.

Regulations originate in the ministry most directly concerned with their subject matter. They need not be reviewed by the Ministry of Justice. They may be reviewed by the Council of Ministers, and generally are so reviewed when they fall into the area of business and commerce. The result of this distinction in process between enactment of legislation and passage of regulations is that the fine points of the rules governing commercial and private life in Cambodia are not easily discernible. A corollary is that these rules are easily subject to change at the behest of ministry officials.

Pursuant to basic principles of socialist legality, the interpretation of the laws is reserved by the Standing Committee of the National Assembly, which is dominated by officers of the executive branch of government. This de facto assignment of the power of interpretation of the laws to the executive branch deprives the judiciary of all institutional power as a branch of government. Not only does the

Cambodian judiciary not have the power of judicial review of the constitutionality of the laws passed by the legislature, but it also does not even have the power to interpret these laws.

The central legislative enactments of the State of Cambodia are described immediately below. Until 1992, when a spate of legislation appeared, they could have been counted on the fingers of one hand. These pre-1992 legislative enactments included the law of organization of the courts creating the courts of first instance and their attached procuracies (1982), the law of organization of the Supreme Court and the Office of the Procurator-General (1985), the law of marriage and the family (1989), and the foreign investment law (1989).

The most significant piece of legislation that appeared in 1992 was a land law. The land law, to be administered by the Ministry of Agriculture, formally established the principle that real property can be individually and privately owned. The right to private ownership is derived from the state, which, in theory, initially held title to all land in Cambodia. The state, however, has decided to divide up the land and give it to the people for their individual ownership, so that they may leave it to their children or sell it. Claims to ownership in land that originated before 1979 are not recognized by the SOC. The ownership rights of those who have owned real property since 1979 are confirmed.

Following close on the heels of the land law in terms of importance to the Cambodian economy was a labor code, governing the rights and obligations of employers and employees. This piece of 1992 legislation, to be administered by the Ministry of Labor and Social Action, regulates labor unions, establishes the duties of employers to their workers, assigns the responsibility for injuries in the workplace, provides for maternity leaves, and regulates dangerous work such as that in the mines.

The greatest number of pieces of legislation passed in 1992 were devoted to matters of finance. A law setting up a national treasury was passed, as were laws authorizing the creation of banks and insurance companies, and a law governing foreign exchange matters. Another piece of legislation, an oddity to Western eyes, created a Ministry of Religions, regulating all organized religion, ranging from Buddhism to Roman Catholicism, in Cambodia.

The area of commercial and business law, untouched by the legislative flurry of 1992, remains dominated by regulations and decrees. The only significant piece of legislation is the foreign investment law of 1989, which is the only one of all the SOC's laws to have been translated into English.[32] The foreign investment law is supplemented by a document titled "Directive regarding Application of the Foreign Investment Law" and a decree on import-export taxes. Another decree law, on contract and civil responsibility, was promulgated in 1988. A commercial code is in the final stages of the drafting process; promulgation is expected by the end of 1992. Laws regulating labor and insurance are in progress.

Criminal procedure is delineated in Decree No. 27, of 1986, and the criminal procedure law of 1989. Decree No. 27, which has been translated into English,[33] sets forth the law of detention and arrest. The criminal procedure law details trial procedure, including the provision of certain procedural safeguards for criminal defendants. The area of substantive criminal law is governed by Decree No. 2, issued in 1980. Decree No. 2 consists of twelve short articles, three of which are concerned with counterrevolutionary crimes. Enforcement of the portions of Decree No. 2 criminalizing counterrevolutionary crimes is said to have been suspended since the signing of the Paris Agreements in October 1991. A draft penal code had been expected to be promulgated in 1992. Presumably it has been relegated to the back burner by the SNC's adoption of the UNTAC criminal justice rules. Officials within the government say that the draft penal code was essentially a remake of the penal code that was in force during Sihanouk's regime.

Analysis of those pieces of legislation that are either fully or partially translated reveals a strong bias in favor of concepts characteristic of socialist legality. Presumably, in light of the provisions of the Paris Agreements committing all four factions to a legal system built around concepts fundamental to liberal democracy, this bias in favor of socialist legality will not be present in future legislation. A new choice, however, confronts the architects of Cambodia's future legal system: whether, within the confines of liberal democracy, to return to the institutions of the past or to develop new institutions more representative of the present status of Khmer culture and society.

Within Cambodian officialdom two tendencies exist. The younger generation, defined as persons in their thirties and forties, seeks to rebuild Cambodia's economic and legal institutions on models provided by the Asian democracies and the United States. With some major exceptions among individuals at the policy-making level, the older generation, educated by and having held power under the French, tends to favor reinstatement of French law and legal institutions. Its attitude derives not so much from a feeling that French institutions are superior as from a sense that, in light of Cambodia's limited resources, the French path is the easier to follow. Even among this group there is a great desire for information about non-French models.

The major legal models that have influenced development around the world are those provided by the Western European nations of England, France, Germany, and Spain, by the United States, and in modern Asia, by Japan. In the past decade a great deal of interest has arisen in the mixed Asian-Anglo-American-Western European legal institutions of the newly industrialized and highly successful Asian economies of Hong Kong, Korea, Singapore, Taiwan, and Thailand. The influence of these models varies according to field of law. The relatively new legal traditions of the United States have been most influential in the field of constitutional law. The much older legal traditions of France and Germany have strongly influenced the fields of civil law and commercial law, respectively.

A distinction exists between commercial and business law on the one hand and constitutional and procedural law on the other. The international trend toward uniformity, or at least similarity, in the commercial and business laws of nations having a market economy narrows the choices for Cambodia in these fields. International conventions strongly influenced by Germanic and Anglo-American notions of contract, commercial, financial, and intellectual property law, conventions to which most nations are signatories, increasingly preempt the field of domestic law. International business negotiations in Asia are often conducted in the English language within a legal framework regulated by these same international conventions. In short, the core content of a course in the modern international business and commercial law relevant to Cambodia would be much the same regardless of the nationality of the teacher.

The situation in the area of constitutional law, criminal justice, and judicial and prosecutorial process is more complex. In this area, too, a synthesis of the Western European, Anglo-American, and Asian legal traditions is in the making, but it is as yet in the early stages. Worldwide, and especially in Asia, the constitutional, judicial, and criminal justice processes of the liberal democracies provide a rich proliferation of alternatives rather than, as yet, converge on a single path.

The French legal tradition has irrevocably shaped the nature of Cambodia's legal and political institutions and will continue to play a major role in its future development. If Cambodia is to join the ranks of the new Asian democracies, however, it must do more than return to the institutions of its immediately postcolonial past. It must look to the institutions of all the liberal democracies of the modern world, both in Asia and in the West.

A Matter of Priorities

Difficult as it is for a Westerner to believe, the international flow of information in the constitutional, criminal, and procedural legal fields has not reached Cambodia. Those persons in policy-making positions within Cambodia do not have access to the ideas that have informed the choices of their Asian neighbors, such as Korea, Singapore, and Thailand. The Khmer Rouge destroyed not only the people who formed the educated class, but also the books from which their knowledge was derived. The Cambodian government has made the fighting of the war a higher priority than the printing of books and the restoration of the higher educational system. Printed material and educated persons are only now beginning to trickle back into Cambodia. In short, Cambodia is in danger of being deprived of the healthy competition between political, legal, and economic ideas that has proved so beneficial to the other new Asian democracies.

It is against this backdrop of an almost complete vacuum of information that the Cambodians have begun to make choices that will determine the nature of their country's political and legal institutions for the generation to come. They want and need information about the options available to them. If information about the legal and political institutions of modern liberal democracies is made available to responsible persons at the policy-making levels of government, Cambodia will almost certainly begin to move toward a Cambodian version of the mixed Asian-Anglo-American-Western European systems characteristic of the new Asian democracies. If that information is not provided, a re-creation of the political and legal institutions of Cambodia's immediate postcolonial past is in the offing. The clock will have turned back more than twenty years.

The theme of reeducation has been present throughout this assessment of the Cambodian legal system, for reeducation in a new legal tradition, that of liberal democracy, is necessary at all levels of government. Whether the Cambodians choose to model their new legal system on France, Japan, Thailand, or the United States, or none of these, a condition precedent to legal reconstruction in Cambodia will be the education and training of persons capable of making a system of law function. As a matter of first priority, the Cambodians must decide what percentage of their limited financial and personnel resources they are willing to devote to this educational program.

There are many persons within the Cambodian government who would welcome the sort of reeducation calculated to facilitate the creation of a political and legal system along liberal democratic lines. These persons can be found in the Supreme National Council, in the ministries and economic institutions of the government of the Phnom Penh regime, in the National Assembly, in the educational system, in the judiciary, in the procuracy, and even in the police. Taken together, they fall into one of two categories: either high-level political, legal, and economic policymakers within the Cambodian government or legal professionals, engaged in the day-to-day administration of the courts, but highly enough placed to have the power to mandate the structural, programmatic, and procedural reforms necessary to implement the policy decisions made in the upper reaches of government. This second group of persons, composed of the ranking officers of the judiciary, the procuracy, and the educational system, will bear the major burden of transforming the Cambodian legal system into a fully functioning democratic system of law, capable of protecting the human rights of citizens. Within the membership of the two groups can be found both the political power to mandate reform and the human resources to implement the reforms mandated. What is lacking is information about available constitutional and legal   alternatives.

The education and training of the Cambodian judiciary is a first step toward the building of the institutional self-identity necessary to an independent judiciary. A judiciary that perceives itself as professional and competent is more likely to resist demands made upon it, in the name of politics or financial gain, for cooperation in the rendering of judgments. Although the Cambodian judiciary, having neither the power of judicial review of the laws for constitutionality nor that of interpretation of the laws, cannot be expected to redefine through its decisions the laws of Cambodia, it does have the potential to provide on a case-by-case basis significant protection for the individual rights of Cambodian citizens. An independent judiciary is essential to the proper functioning of a democratic society. Few tasks in the area of democratic reform are more important than establishing the independence of the Cambodian judiciary.

An independent judiciary, working with a procuracy reconceived as the representative of the law enforcement arm of the executive branch of government, will be better able to control the Cambodian police. Control of the police is critical to enforcement of constitutional and legislative guarantees of human rights. Although control of the police is ultimately the responsibility of the ministers of the interior and of national security, the ability and willingness of judges and procurators to correct and deter police abuses of power play no small part in creating a climate of social and political expectations that the police will abide by the law. Human rights violations will continue in Cambodia until the Cambodian police are taught to respect the law.

Cambodia's legal institutions are so recently created, some still on paper or in operation for five years or less, that they have not had the time to become set in socialist ways. Because of the specialized nature of law, the government has perforce selected many of the persons who administer the legal system on the basis of level of education achieved and learning capacity rather than on the basis of political correctness. The legal system is supervised and staffed by some of the most able members of Cambodian officialdom. If these reformers are not sabotaged by enemies in rival factions within the government, they should be able to bring Cambodia's legal system through the difficult passages that await it. The dismantling of Cambodia's socialist political and legal institutions has begun. The debate over the nature of their replacements has also begun. The new political and legal system is intended to be in place, if only in outline form, by the 1993 elections.

Notes

1. The author acknowledges Ken Bingham, Richard Blue, Margaret Carpenter, Trina Grillo, Thelton Henderson, Larry Serra, Craig Steffensen, and Stephanie Wildman for their comments on early drafts of this article, Run Saray for his documentary support and translation of modern Cambodian legislation, and the Asia Foundation for its support of research.

2. For discussions of socialist legality, see Harold J. Berman, *Justice in the U.S.S.R.* (New York: Vintage Books, 1950): 13-170; William E. Butler, *Soviet Law* (London: Butterworth's, 1983): 26-38; S. Leng and H. Chiu, *Criminal Justice in Post-Mao China* (Albany: University of New York Press, 1983): 9-28; Donovan, "The Structure of the Chinese Criminal Justice System: A Comparative Perspective," *University of San Francisco Law Review* 21 (1987): 229, 289-91.

3. The term *government of Cambodia* is, owing to Cambodia's political situation, necessarily imprecise. Until the United Nations-supervised elections of 1993, the question of who, or which political faction, controls Cambodia will not be finally resolved. UNTAC and the government of the State of Cambodia, which controls most

government institutions inside Cambodia, and the Supreme National Council, the repository of Cambodia's sovereignty for international diplomatic purposes, are involved in the rebuilding of the country's legal system. At the time of this writing, in early 1992, the interest of the Supreme National Council is mainly in the constitution-writing process. The government of the State of Cambodia, on the other hand, through the Hun Sen regime in Phnom Penh, has been actively involved in the reconstruction of all aspects of Cambodia's legal system. In this essay the term *government* refers to the government of the State of Cambodia unless otherwise indicated.

4. *Procuracy* is a term derived from the French word *procurateur*, which means prosecutor. The term *procuracy* is used, in some legal traditions, usually socialist, to refer to the prosecutorial resources of a nation, just as the term *judiciary* is used to refer to the judicial resources of a nation.

5. See *Les Constitutions d'Asie et d'Australie* (Ouvrage Publié sous la direction, avec une preface et des notices, de Henri Puget) (Paris: Editions de l'Epargne, 1965): 159-61; Bowen and Ross, "Cambodia: Democratic Kampuchea," in *Constitutions of the Countries of the World*, ed. A.P. Blaustein and G.H. Flanz (1989): ii.

6. See articles 25, 49, 74, 96, 97, and 114 of the Constitution du Royaume du Cambodge, July 1959, Phnom Penh, 1962, in *Les Constitutions d'Asie et d'Australie*, 162-77. For the 1956 amendments discussed below, see articles 3-16 and 92-45.

7. See Constitution de la Republique Khmere du 10 mai, 1972 (author's files).

8. For an English translation of the 1976 constitution, see A. P. Blaustein and G. H. Flanz, eds., *Constitutions of the Countries of the World* (1989).

9. 1976 Constitution of Democratic Kampuchea, article 10, in *Constitutions of the Countries of the World*, ed. A.P. Blaustein and G.H. Flanz (1989).

10. For an English translation of the 1989 constitution of the State of Cambodia, see A. P. Blaustein and G. H. Flanz, eds., *Constitutions of the Countries of the World* (1989). For an English translation of the 1981 constitution of the People's Republic of Kampuchea, see the

Federal Broadcast Information Service (FBIS:IV) report of July 1, 1981. For a discussion of the 1981 constitution, see Frances Starner, "Next: A Name Without Shame," *AsiaWeek*, 27 March 1981.

11. A 1989 decree law recognized the right to ownership of real and personal property.

12. Closing speech at the Extraordinary Congress of the Cambodian People's Party, 18 October 1991.

13. Agreements on a Comprehensive Political Settlement of the Cambodian Conflict, part VII, Principles for a New Constitution for Cambodia, annex 5, paragraphs 1-6, in Final Act of the Paris Conference on Cambodia, 23 October 1991.

14. Ibid., part I, Arrangements During the Transitional Period, article 6.

15. Ibid., annex 1 (UNTAC Mandate), section (b) (Civil Administration), paragraph 5(b); see also ibid., annex 1 (UNTAC Mandate), section (b) (Civil Administration), paragraph 6.

16. Ibid., annex 1 (UNTAC Mandate), section (d) (Elections), paragraph 3(a).

17. Ibid., annex 1 (UNTAC Mandate), section (d) (Elections), paragraph 3(b).

18. The current government relies heavily on the two remaining judges who survived the Khmer Rouge massacres for advice on matters relating to legislation, the courts, and the legal system generally. These men have been charged with, among many other duties, the responsibility of reforming legal education along liberal democratic lines.

19. An interdisciplinary approach to the teaching of law is characteristic not only of socialist legal education but also of European legal education at the undergraduate level.

20. The French tradition has been perpetuated by the few surviving French-trained Cambodian lawyers who have been placed in charge of legal education. For example, Loeung Chhay, the director of the Institute of Public Administration and Law, did graduate work in France.

21. Until 1991 the University of Phnom Penh functioned solely as a teacher-training institute; all of its graduates were required to

become secondary-school teachers. Beginning in the academic year 1992-93, it will become a "true" university, educating students for more general purposes in the liberal arts and sciences. The University of Phnom Penh now has eight thousand students, divided between the liberal arts, social sciences, science, and the pharmacy school.

22. Lawyers' Committee for Human Rights, *Cambodia: The Justice System and Violations of Human Rights* (New York: Lawyers' Committee for Human Rights, 1992); Amnesty International, *State of Cambodia: Human Rights Developments: 1 October 1991 to 31 January 1992* (New York: Amnesty International); Lawyers' Committee for Human Rights, *Kampuchea: After the Worst* (New York: Lawyers' Committee for Human Rights, 1985). James D. Ross's excellent report for the Lawyers' Committee appeared after this essay had been submitted for publication. It contains a great deal of detailed material on the SOC criminal justice system that will be of interest to lawyers and other persons concerned with the nature and quality of criminal justice and human rights protection, or lack thereof, in Cambodia.

23. The UNTAC rules of criminal law and procedure require the creation of a court of appeal.

24. Interview of November 29, 1991, with prosecutors attached to the Office of the Procurator-General.

25. Decree Law No. 27, Arrest, Detention, Temporary Imprisonment, Release, and Search of Domicile, Property, and Person (1986), translated in Michael Vickery, "Criminal Law in the People's Republic of Kampuchea," *Journal of Contemporary Asia* 17 (1987).

26. Article 60(2) of the 1989 constitution of the State of Cambodia provides that the Council of State has the duty of issuing decrees. The chairman of the Council of State is the supreme commander of the Cambodian People's Armed Forces and chairman of the National Defense Council.

27. The only authoritative pronouncement on the right of land ownership is to be found in the 1992 land law, which provides that Cambodians have the right to own, to use, and to inherit land.

28. This list was derived from interviews with the personnel of

various ministries. The constitution provides that "the Council of State, the Council of Ministers, the chairman of the National Assembly, [assorted mass organizations], the president of the People's Supreme Court, and the Prosecutor General attached to the People's Supreme Court have the right to draft a bill for the National Assembly." 1989 Constitution of the State of Cambodia, article 53.

29. "The Council of Ministers is the government of the State of Cambodia . . . and is responsible to the National Assembly and the Council of State and reports on its activities to these organs." 1989 Constitution of the State of Cambodia, article 64. "The Council of Ministers has the following functions: (1) To draft laws and other bills for recommendation to the National Assembly and the Council of State . . . (7) To suspend the implementation of, revise, or annul inappropriate conventions and directives of ministers and chairmen of various state institutions, and suspend the implementation of, revise, or annul inappropriate decisions and directives of people's committees at all levels. . . ." Ibid., article 66.

30. "The Standing Committee of the National Assembly has the following duties: (1) Organize National Assembly sessions. (2) Convene ordinary or extraordinary sessions. (3) Interpret laws. (4) Inititate draft laws." Ibid., article 49/2.

31. Ibid., article 54. Constitutional amendments must be approved by a two-thirds majority.

32. The foreign investment law of 1989 was translated into English by Phat Mau, under the supervision of H. Lawrence Serra. This translation appears in *East Asian Executive Reports*, 15 October 1990. For discussions of the foreign investment law, see H. L. Serra, "Cambodia's Foreign Investment Law," *East Asian Executive Reports*, 15 September 1990, 10; "Cambodia's Law on Foreign Investment," *California State Bar International Law Section Newsletter* (Fall 1990).

33. Michael Vickery, "Criminal Law in the People's Republic of Kampuchea," *Journal of Contemporary Asia* 17 (1987).

Appendix

Excerpts From

SECOND PROGRESS REPORT OF THE SECRETARY-GENERAL ON THE UNITED NATIONS TRANSITIONAL AUTHORITY IN CAMBODIA

UNITED NATIONS DOCUMENT S/24578

21 SEPTEMBER 1992

[From "I. Progress Made to Date in the Implementation of Resolutions 745 (1992) and 766 (1992) and Tasks Still to be Performed"]

2. UNTAC is now close to full deployment throughout almost the whole territory of Cambodia. However, the continuing refusal of the Party of Democratic Kampuchea (PDK) to grant UNTAC personnel access to the zones it controls or to commit its forces to cantonment as called for in the implementation plan (S/23613) gives grounds for serious concern. As explained in my second special report, PDK has introduced its own interpretations of the provisions of the Paris Agreements relating to the verification of the withdrawal and non-return of foreign forces and to the role and powers of the Supreme National Council (see S/23177, annex). PDK asserts that these provisions have not been implemented and that, until they are, it is not in a position to proceed with the implementation of the other provisions. In line with this assertion, PDK has issued a series of proposals laying down conditions under which it would be prepared to participate fully in the peace process. Although my Special Representative has carefully studied all these proposals with a view to identifying ways of accommodating PDK's concerns, it has not been possible to accept them because they are inconsistent with the Paris Agreements.

3. In other respects, however, the implementation of the mission is proceeding apace. The electoral law was adopted on 5 August 1992. Provisional registra-

tion of political parties has begun and preparations are under way for the registration of voters. It is still intended that elections will be held not later than May 1993. The repatriation of refugees and displaced persons is making steady progress; more than 115,000 had returned to Cambodia by 15 September 1992 without serious incident. The progressive installation of United Nations civilian officials in the administrative structures of the three Cambodian parties that are complying with the peace process has enabled UNTAC to establish supervision and control in accordance with its mandate. The work of the human rights and civilian police components has been extended to every province. A number of rehabilitation assistance programmes have been approved by the Supreme National Council.

[From "II. Conclusions and Recommendations"]

65. UNTAC has made substantial strides towards its goal in the six months since its inception despite constraints imposed by the refusal of PDK to participate fully in the peace process, in particular the second phase of the cease-fire. Following the adoption of the electoral law, provisional registration of parties has begun and registration of voters is about to begin. Extensive military deployment across most of the country and a strong police presence extending to the village level have been established. More than 115,000 refugees and displaced persons have been safely repatriated. The international community has pledged $880 million to meet the essential rehabilitation needs of the country. Supervision and control over the existing administrative structures of three of the parties have been established and are being strengthened. UNTAC continues to inform Cambodians of their human rights and to foster the protection of those rights. All UNTAC's activities are becoming increasingly familiar to Cambodians throughout the country as a result of the information and public awareness campaign. UNTAC has thus acquired a powerful momentum that has enabled it to move ahead simultaneously on many fronts. Its presence has already had a profound and probably lasting impact on Cambodia. These achievements would not have been possible without the continuing support of the Security Council and the international community, the full cooperation of His Royal Highness Prince Sihanouk and the positive attitude and goodwill of the great majority of Cambodians.

66. Having carefully reviewed what UNTAC has accomplished so far, as well as the obstacles it has faced, I remain determined that the electoral process should be carried out in accordance with the timetable laid down in the

implementation plan. While the attitude of the PDK has limited implementation of the plan, UNTAC has consistently stressed that the door is still open to PDK to participate fully and constructively in the peace process and that the military component stands ready to undertake the cantonment of NADK forces. My Special Representative has also made it clear that, in accordance with the Paris Agreements, UNTAC must be given unhindered access to PDK-controlled areas and that all its components must be allowed to operate as required in those areas in order to discharge their respective functions.

67. Meanwhile, UNTAC will press forward with the implementation of all the provisions of the Paris Agreements, including those concerning the verification of withdrawal and non-return of foreign forces and the cessation of outside military assistance to the Cambodian parties. This may require an increase in the number of checkpoints within the country and along the boarders with one or more of the neighboring countries, as well as appropriate modifications in the manning of those checkpoints and an updating of their terms of reference. More intensive military investigations and patrols may also be required.

68. That said, the persistent failure of the PDK to meet the obligations it assumed when it signed the Paris Agreements obstructs the full implementation of those Agreements. The present drift in the peace process cannot be allowed to continue without seriously impairing UNTAC's ability to carry out its mandate within the time-frame set by the Security Council. It is clear that the time is approaching when some difficult decisions regarding ways and means of pursuing this operation will have to be seriously considered. Naturally such decisions should be taken only when the international community is satisfied that every effort to resolve the present difficulties has been made. UNTAC will therefore continue to work closely with the parties and the Supreme National Council to identify possible solutions within the framework of the Paris Agreements.

69. For UNTAC to achieve its objectives, the continuing support of the international community, particularly of neighboring countries as called for in resolution 766 (1992), will be invaluable, not least in helping to communicate to the leadership of PDK the firm resolve of the United Nations that UNTAC should implement its mandate vigorously and to the full. The support of the Security Council itself is of special importance. The Council may wish to take further action to impress upon the parties the international community's firm determination to press ahead with the implementation of the settlement, so as to bring peace to Cambodia and enable the Cambodian people to look to a better and more stable future.

70. In this connection, I intend, subject to the approval of the Security Council, to request the co-Chairmen of the Paris Conference to undertake, within a definite time-frame, consultations as provided for by article 29 of the Paris Agreements. These consultations would be carried out in close cooperation with myself and my Special Representative, with the aim of finding a way out of the present impasse or, if that should prove impossible, exploring appropriate steps to ensure the realization of the fundamental objective of the Paris Agreements.

A Guide to Acronyms

The Phnom Penh Regime

SOC	State of Cambodia, its current name.
PRK	People's Republic of Kampuchea, regime's name, 1979-89.
KPRP	Khmer People's Revolutionary Party, ruling political party, 1979-92.
CPP	Cambodian People's Party, the KPRP's current name.

Resistance and Individual Factions

KR	Khmer Rouge.
DK	Democratic Kampuchea, KR regime in power, 1975-78.
DKP	Democratic Kampuchea Party, current name of KR political party.
NADK	National Army of Democratic Kampuchea, KR military.
CGDK	Coalition Government of Democratic Kampuchea, 1982-90.
FUNCINPEC	National United Front for an Independent, Neutral, Peaceful and Cooperative Cambodia (from French acronym), political party of Norodom Ranarridh.
ANS	Armee Nationale Sihanoukiste, its military arm.
KPNLF	Khmer People's National Liberation Front.
NCR	Noncommunist resistance.

The United Nations Perm 5 Plan and Other International Terms

UNTAC	United Nations Transitional Authority in Cambodia.
SNC	Supreme National Council.
PICC	Paris International Conference on Cambodia.
ASEAN	Association of Southeast Asian Nations.
JIM	Jakarta Informal Meetings.
UNHCR	United Nations High Commissioner for Refugees.
UNDP	United Nations Development Programme.
UNICEF	United Nations Children's Fund.
UNBRO	United Nations Border Relief Organization.
NGO	Nongovernmental organization.

About the Authors

Dolores A. Donovan is professor of law at the University of San Francisco and since 1989 Director of the Asian Pacific Legal Studies Program at the university's school of law. Professor Donovan is a specialist in comparative constitutional law and criminal justice systems, with an emphasis on human rights. Her current research concentrates on Asian legal systems. Professor Donovan received her A.B. and J.D. from Stanford University. She is the author of a book on the ethical responsibilities of judges and prosecutors in the California criminal justice system and of articles and essays on American and Chinese criminal law and procedure.

Sidney Jones has been executive director of Asia Watch since 1989, following four years as a researcher in the Asia and Pacific department of Amnesty International in London. From 1977 to 1984 she worked with the Ford Foundation in Jakarta, Indonesia, and New York as a program officer in the Developing Countries Program. A specialist on Southeast Asia, she has published numerous articles on Islam in Indonesia and on human rights issues in Cambodia, Indonesia, the Philippines, and China. A summa cum laude graduate of the University of Pennsylvania, Ms. Jones received her M.A. from the same university.

Robert J. Muscat is senior economist at the Institute for Policy Reform, in Washington, D.C., and a visiting scholar at the East Asian Institute of Columbia University. He has served as economics adviser to the Thai government's development planning agency, the Undersecretary for Economics in the Malaysian Ministry of Finance, and as program policy director for the UN Development Programme. In the

U.S. Agency for International Development he has held positions in Southeast Asian, Latin American, and African missions, including USAID's chief economist in 1972-75, and has consulted for the World Bank and UNICEF. His recent publications include *Thailand and the United States: Development, Security and Foreign Aid* and *Cambodia: Post-Settlement Reconstruction.*

Dinah Pokempner is a graduate of Yale University and received her J.D. degree from Columbia Law School in 1989. She was admitted to the New York State Bar in 1992. As an Orville Schell Fellow at Human Rights Watch in 1990-91, she carried out research on the situation of Vietnamese refugees in Hong Kong. In 1992 she became a research associate for Asia Watch on Cambodia and Vietnam and wrote the 1992 Asia Watch report titled *Human Rights, Political Control, and the UN Mission in Cambodia.*

Frederick Z. Brown is a fellow at the Johns Hopkins Foreign Policy Institute and directs Southeast Asian studies at the Paul H. Nitze School of Advanced International Studies. A former Department of State foreign service officer, he served in France, Thailand, the Soviet Union, Vietnam, and Cyprus. From 1984 to 1987 he was professional staff member for East Asia and the Pacific on the U.S. Senate Foreign Relations Committee. He is author of *Second Chance: The United States and Indochina in the 1990s.*

THE JOHNS HOPKINS FOREIGN POLICY INSTITUTE

George Packard
Dean, School of Advanced International Studies
Acting Chairman, FPI

Michael Green
Associate Executive Director

William Bader Fellow	**Arthur Hartman** Diplomat-in-Residence	**Walter Slocombe** Fellow
Frederick Z. Brown Fellow	**Hisayoshi Ina** Fellow	**Hedrick Smith** Editor-in-Residence
Charles H. Fairbanks, Jr. Fellow	**Wilfrid L. Kohl** Director, International Energy Program	
Joseph Fromm Fellow	**Peter Rodman** Fellow	**I. William Zartman** Director, Program on Conflict Management

The Johns Hopkins Foreign Policy Institute (FPI) was established in 1980 as an integral part of the Paul H. Nitze School of Advanced International Studies (SAIS) in Washington, D.C., to unite the worlds of scholarship and public affairs in the search for realistic answers to contemporary problems facing the United States. The FPI is a meeting place for SAIS faculty members and students, as well as for government analysts, policymakers, diplomats, journalists, business leaders, and other specialists in international affairs.

FPI sponsors numerous research projects on current world problems and organizes teaching in a variety of fields, including security studies and international energy policy. Members of the institute include the entire SAIS faculty. Also associated with the institute are numerous experts from the fields of diplomacy, business, journalism, politics, government, as well as other universities and research organizations.

The Foreign Policy Institute publishes the student-edited and student-managed *SAIS Review*. a semi-annual journal on foreign affairs. The institute has also established a monograph series that presents the best in current research and analysis taking place at FPI. These books and other publications examine topics ranging from the evolution of U.S. strategic policy to international terrorism to the structure of security policy-making in the former Soviet Union. Other publications include *Policy Consensus Reports*, which present recommendations on a series of critical foreign policy issues; and *SAIS Energy Papers*, presenting new research on international energy resource issues.

For additional information, write to: Director of Publications, The Paul H. Nitze School of Advanced International Studies, The Johns Hopkins Foreign Policy Institute, 1619 Massachusetts Avenue, N.W., Washington, D.C. 20036-2297.